The Poetry of Bert Padell
Including the poems from
"Bert's Words" and "Hey Babes"

Designed by Victor Zurbel
Photography by Joel Markman

Library of Congress Cataloging-in-Publication Data
Padell, Bert:
  1. Collected Poems of Bert Padell
  2. Poetry

ISBN:
0-9624946-0-7 Hardbound
0-9624946-1-5 Paperback

Published by Sparks Publishing Company,
217 East 85th Street, Suite 101, New York, N.Y. 10028
Direct all correspondence and inquiries to this address.

First Edition 1990

Designed by Victor Zurbel
Photography by Joel Markman

DEDICATION

To Bobby, my Sweet P, my wife, my love.

To Ellie, Scott, Wendy, David and Randi
the loves of my life, my children.

Always a thank you to the late Montgomery Clift
and the late Jack E. Jensen.

Thanks to Armand and Mario, Shep
for your love and friendship.

To Elizabeth Greco, love and thanks.

To all, to have sweet harmony, love,
peace, health and tranquility.

To my partners and fellow people who
I work with. Thank you for your confidence,
respect, intelligence and sweet love.

Special thank you to my friend, client, my
artist who made this book possible, Peter Max.

With special due to Victor Zurbel for his
work on this book.

CLIENT LIST

Madonna
Cyndi Lauper
Luther Vandross
Peter Max
Mary Lambert
Alice Cooper
Faye Dunaway
David McCallum
Andie MacDowell
August Darnell
Roddy Piper
Bitten
Paulina Porizkova
Phil Ramone
Jackie Mason
Jyll Rosenfeld
Joan Jett
Vinnie Bell
Oren "Juice" Jones
Larry Smith
Larry Blackmon
Laura Morton
The System
Carl Williams
Veruschka Von
  Lehndorff
Cyndy Garvey
Andrew Goldmark
Andy Panda
Fonzi Thorton
Slick Rick
Alyson Williams
Eric B & Rakim
Hinton Battle
Obba Babatunde
Colonel Abrams
Kurtis Blow
Run DMC
Whodini
Talking Heads

John "Jellybean"
  Benitez
Aaron Russo
Little Steven
Stephen Bray
Franke Previte
Sally Kirkland
Lou Piniella
Gerald Diduck
David Brooks
Robert DeNiro
Davey Dee
Louis Vega
EPMD
LeMel Humes
Billy Chinnock
Midnight Star
Steven Gadd
Al B Sure
Fernando Saunders
Dayle Haddon
Lisa Fisher
Robert Fraboni
Stephanie Roman
Noel Pagen
Margaret Whitton
Francoise Nars
Pamela Geiger
Laura Branigan
Tommy Jenkins
Ace Frehley
Cameo
Nathan Leftenant
Freddy Bastone
Pat DiNizio
Lennie Petze
Taylor Dane
Rusty Staub
Freddie Gershon
Jon Vickers

Bonnie Pointer
Starpoint
Paul Blair
Art Rust Jr.
Joey Mills
Nick Lowe
Elvis Costello
Riviera Global
Graham Parker
David Fishof
David Wolff
Shep Gordon
Will Botwin
Rosie Vela Roberts
Law and Order
Big Daddy Kane
Gary Kurfirst
Russell Simmons
Lyor Cohen
John Vikers
Davie Dee
Vincent Bell
Paul Young
Alison Moyet
Rick Derringer
Randy Myer
Biz Markie
Ernest Bryner
Marita Stavrou
Khadija Adam
Ashley Richardson
Trixie
Mark Berry
Jerry Powers
Brett Lover
Freddy Foxxx
Dongie Fresh
Lorraine Brocca
Key West
The Pasadenas

BERT PADELL- "ACCOUNTANT TO THE STARS"

To many people in the entertainment industry, Bert Padell is known as "the accountant to the stars".

But in addition to his talent for balancing numbers, Bert Padell also has an extraordinary talent for capturing thoughts and putting them into poetry. From his unique vantage point, across the desk from many of the world's greatest entertainers, performers, sports figures and artists, Padell sees beneath the public image to the very humanity of the person, with all of his or her strengths and weaknesses, hopes and fears, and joys and sorrows.

Here in "Thoughts", his third volume of poetry (including his two previous books, "Bert's Words", 1976, and "Hey Babes", 1985), are a fascinating collection of the uncommon perceptions and deeply felt emotions which mark this unusual complex man.

Born in the Bronx, Padell originally intended to become a baseball player and served as Yankee batboy during the team's glory years, while also beginning to amass a priceless collection of baseball memorabillia. But when injury curtailed his budding baseball career, he pursued law and accounting with equal energy and verve, building a prestigious accounting firm on Broadway. As Joe DiMaggio once said in a letter,"...In both baseball and business, Bert Padell has exhibited a sure eye, a steady hand, and can still tell the difference between a curve or a sinker whether it comes from the pitching mound or the stock market."

Walking into Bert Padell's office, one is awed by the enormous array of antique clocks, paintings, gold and platinum records, movie posters, baseball treasures and other objects that fill every square inch of the huge space.

Similarly, on opening the pages of "Thoughts", one cannot fail to be impressed by the vast array of perceptions and observations that are captured in his poetry. No matter how important or trivial something might seem to the rest of us, there is beauty enough in it to be recorded and shared by the eyes and heart of the poet Bert Padell.

INDEX OF POEMS AND THEIR DESCRIPTIONS

A DARING MAN	About a man I thought I knew from California	98
A DINNER WITH FRIENDS	Dinner with five true friends: Jim Buck, Alice Buck, Jay Kirshenbaum, Carol Kirshenbaum, and my wife Bobby.	404
A DOLLAR FOR JAMIE	To Buddy & Lorrell Morgan-- in tribute to their late son	231
A FATHER, A SON, A FRIEND	To James Malloy, David Malloy and Even Stevens-- father, son and friend-- producers & songwriters together	82
AFFAIR OF LIFE	Always having a love affair with my love, Bobby	348
AFRAID TO BE HURT	A person having a new relationship and fearing the old- especially of being hurt	314
A FRIENDSHIP	A friendship separated by miles apart	59
A GARDEN OF TREES	Trees on the Major Deagan Expressway	153
A GIRL CALLED ALI	To a former client and friend, Ali McGraw, when she was a fashion model	40
A LADY CHASING THE WIND	A client and a dear friend, Faye Dunaway	37
ALICE AND SHEP	To friends and stars in their own way-- Alice Cooper and Shep Gordon	77
ALL THE SAME	We as it is-- are all the same	352
ALONE	One's feelings to be alone	388
ALWAYS WITH ME	Though miles may separate us, my love Bobby is always with me	360
A MAN I MET	I met a man-- in my thoughts-- who finally became Freddie Gershon, Esq.	360
A MAN NAMED FRANK	To Frank Sinatra-- thoughts from his friend and mine, the late Montgomery Clift	139
A MAN OF HIS TOILS	About a former client, film director and film producer- Jerry Ansel	184

A MAN OF LOVE	To my friend and client and great artist, Peter Max	89
A MAN'S CRISIS	To an IRS agent, wherever he may be	180
AN EMPTY FEELING	The love of my friend's father, Louis Picker, for my friend Eddie Picker	59
A-PART	Living away from one's love	318
A PARTING LOVE	When your love falls out	338
A PASSING YEAR	Years pass and the best is to come	364
A PUZZLEMENT OF LIFE	Life is like a puzzle	300
ASK BUT WHY	The question-- why things happen?	230
A SONG OF LIFE	To love someone dear	26
A STRANGER I NEVER KNEW	About my departed father, Irving	206
A SUMMER END	Waiting for summer-- Then summer	286
AT A FUNERAL	How one feels and regrets to be at a funeral	188
AT LEAST YOU TRIED	Trying to do something/ winning is of no importance/ just trying	141
A TRAGEDY OF LIFE	A sudden death, the killing by one, accidently	354
A TRIBUTE	To a former Yankee baseball player- the late Thurman Munson	152
AUCTION OF LIFE	Life is like going to an auction-- and what happens	340
A VILLAGE	A village is Club Med which I went to	220
A WORD	Fame and wealth thanks you-- what to expect	375
BEAR FRUITFUL THOUGHTS	Bearing good thoughts or another while casting bad ones on me	333
BE FRIENDS	A wife accepting her husband with that of her father	402
BEING ANGRY	What I should be at times, thank you, Peter Parcher for your help	165
BEN	My good friend - Ben Vereen	63

BRING US TOGETHER	Uniting us together-- Our country	339
BUT FOR LOVE	Love, and its meaning to us all	55
CHALLENGE OF OUR LIFE	The tragedy of the space ship-- Challenger VII	384
DEATH ITSELF	A friend's death and what it means to me	347
DEBORAH	A poem about Debby Harry of Blondie	51
DONALD	About a fashion model and her lover photographer	223
DON'T TOUCH	To love someone, yet to have to wait	333
ENJOY	To enjoy what we have	25
EXPOSED TO YOU	Having someone caring and exposed to them	371
FAREWELL TO A DREAM	A dream vanishing/ yet why	110
FORGET HIM NOT	Forget not ones that pass away	261
GARLAND	To former client and friend, Garland Jeffries	145
GIVE ME YOUR DREAMS	Especially for my wife Bobby	219
GIVE THANKS	Thanks from me for being	281
GOD SITS ON A PILLOW	To Pete Stingy, a friend and film editor, who died suddenly	304
GOODBYE FOR NOW	Saying goodbye	374
GROWING OLD	The glory of growing old in years	389
HANDS TO HEAVEN	Madonna, and her show in Wembly, England	378
HAVE YOU LIVED?	To say to one's self "Live"	270
HEAVEN ONLY KNOWS	To my late brother-in-law Lawrence Schnuer	254
HER KISS	The feeling of a simple kiss	353
HER LAST CURTAIN	To the late Judy Garland-- Thank you	102
HER LITTLE RED SHOES	Watching a ballet with a dancer with little red shoes	288

HEY JOEY	To a client and friend Joey Mills, make-up artist	93
HIS SONG IS HEARD FOREVER	To the late John Lennon of the Beatles	105
HOMEBOY	A tribute to my friend and client, Kurtis Blow, a music rapper & Russell Simmons, manager & music producer	396
HOW CAN IT HAPPEN AGAIN?	How can the world let what happens, happen... since it happened before ?	177
HOW DOES ONE FEEL FOR LIFE?	The feeling, the wanting of life	276
HOW DO I TELL YOU?	The desire for one to say I love you and want you	368
HOW MUCH CAN ONE TAKE?	How one feels when everything is crowding in	32
I AM WHAT I AM	What all of us are and trying to accept	334
I COULD LOVE YOU	Especially for my wife Bobby	191
I'D DO IT TWICE	What people really think	
IF I HAD KNOWN	A trilogy-- a story of life between a father, a mother, a son in Nazi Germany	175
I FOUND YOU	To Robert DeNiro, my dear friend	410
I GIVE THANKS	Giving thanks to someone you love	245
I HEARD A SOUND	To a former client and group I knew	124
I KISS MY COUNTRY	My feeling toward the USA	328
I KNOW	To know we are one-- each of us without each other-- nothing	125
I LIVE TODAY	To live each day for today	292
I LOVE THEE	A feeling when falling in love	372
I'M COMING HOME	The desire in us all to return to our home	249
I MISS MY SON	To my son Scott and all the sons leaving for summer camp etc.	203
I MUST WRITE HIM A NOTE	Writing someone to tell them what one feels	409

IN DREAMS	Dreaming of love	211
IN FAITH	To believe in God and in faith of believing	262
I NEVER KNEW YOU	To Sarah, my late Grandma	205
I PRAY TO GOD	Praying to God-- and being heard	83
I PUT THE DAY AWAY	Written about a young lady who was very depressed about her day and her life-- Dana Ames	259
I SAW A SHOW	To Broadway and its Broadway shows	113
I STEPHANIE	To Stephanie Mills, my friend	85
I THOUGHT IT WAS YESTERDAY	The feeling that today is really yesterday	390
IT NEVER STOPS	The waves of the ocean and what it does to us	277
IT SAID	To Luther Vandross, God talking to him. Written in Rome, Italy when I was sick	122
ITS USE-- MONEY	Money, and what it does to people	115
I'VE GOT TO BE WHAT I AM	What all of us try to say who we are, but sometimes some of us fail	253
I WANT TO BELIEVE	Found a friend from out in the cold. Ed Germano-- owner of the Hit Factory Music Recording Studios.	390
JUSTICE	Justice and what it is to me	201
LEARN LOVE FROM DEATH	Losing someone dear, yet learning how much you loved them-- only after their death.	346
LITTLE IS ENOUGH	Wanting someone, even though not very much	397
LIVE TO DANCE	To Susan, my former girl-friend who loved to dance	169
LIVE WITH HATE	A trilogy-- a story of life between a father, a mother, a son in Nazi Germany	173
LOOK OF LOVE	To Jeffrey Bowen and Bonnie Pointer-- Jeffrey listening to Bonnie sing	72
LOVE ME	To dream of love and what it is	213

LOVE ME JUST A LITTLE	To be loved just a bit	374
LOVE OR MISBEHAVIN'	About two swell people-- Carole Bayer Sager and Marvin Hamlisch, a former client and friend	117
MAN'S BEST FRIEND IS MAN	The title tells itself-- Man-- what he is to <u>Man</u>	397
ME	To achieve and let it be	402
MEMORIES ARE FUNNY THINGS	When one thinks of the past-- of memories	211
MUST IT BE	What people want and expect, but the feelings of one asking oneself-- Must it Be-- that way	366
MY DESIRE	To Ernie Catanese, my friend-- he is the friend	59
MY FALLEN SENATOR	To the late Senator Robert Kennedy	108
MY FRIEND IS GONE	What a friend is-- and suddenly it changes	310
MY GROUP-- THE PIE	To my rock music group Humble Pie	127
MY LOVE FOR MY FATHER	To my dad I never knew	141
MY OWN TOWN	My feelings about my town-- NYC	324
MY SECRETARY	To my former secretary Lyn Gendler and all the secretaries of the world	224
MY SON, MY SON	I saw a motion picture with Glen Ford who played a father looking for his lost son	338
NEVER THEIR OWN MEN	Men that are just pawns of others	111
NOTHING DIES THAT IS REMEMBERED	The title expresses itself	265
NOTHING IS FOREVER	To the group, the J. Geils Band	264
ODE TO ALLEN	Poem written for old time comedian Fred Allen	288
ONE DAY OLDER	I become one day older in life/ and my feelings and beliefs	183
ONE FEELING	Feeling of something fresh-- a woman	363
ONE MEMORY	To the late actor James Dean	101

OUR LADY	The Statue of Liberty-- its meaning to us	382
OUR MAN DEE	To a music manager Dee Anthony	74
PEOPLE I REPRESENT	The Three Degrees and their manager Richard, October 24, 1979	170
PRECIOUS LOVE	Love-- what it is	280
PRISONERS OF MONEY	All people in the world are prisoners of this entity-- money	187
REMEMBER OUR LOVE	Our love of each other-- Bobby, my wife and myself	60
REMEMBER WHAT I DID	People have a tendency to forget what one does for another	60
SAVE YOUR FRIENDSHIP	Friendship	386
SENSE OF EXCELLENCE	To be number one, is it excellence?	394
SENSITIVITY	What we should all have	35
SHADOWS OF YOUR LIFE	Looking at oneself and one's shadows	251
SHE MUST LEAVE	To June Nadell, my beloved friend and partner's late wife	215
SHOULD HAVE	What we all say	402
SILENCE	A deaf man and the world/its silence to me and others	161
SOON WE WILL BE ONE	My love for my wife Bobby	312
SORRY	The need at times to say Sorry for doing...	290
SO YOUNG	To my beloved wife and friend, Bobby	31
STONE FACES	The Tombstones in East Hampton by the lake	405
SWEET LOVE OF MINE	Feelings that become so sweet	320
SWEETNESS OF MY LOVES	To wife Bobby and my three children, Ellen, Scott and Wendy	56
SWEETNESS OF SUCCESS	What we strive to become part of	197
SWIFTNESS OF LOVE	When I feel in love with Bobby, my wife	210

TALKING WORDS	Mere talking-- but the words I speak, I mean	388
TEARS IN THE RAIN	Inspired by sorrow and happiness of various events on television and in newspapers-- and what tears can bring to these events	408
TEDDY	To Teddy Pendergrass, singer and entertainer and friend-- and the hurt of his accident which he is overcoming	137
THANK GOD IT IS NOT MINE	My daughter Ellen's friend died at the age of 8 many years ago. Her name -- Michelle Zaroff	199
THANKS FOR THE CHANCE	To a gentleman, L.P., who gave me a chance-- Thanks	157
THE AIR OF DEFEAT	From defeat stems success	353
THE AWARD	The feelings involved for the CARS during their nominations for GRAMMY	70
THE BACK END	To my friends, the Truck Driver	83
THE BAND	Dr. Buzzard and the Original Savannah Band	95
THE BETRAYERS	A March 31st I will never forget	239
THE BIG FELLOW	About the one and only John "DUKE" Wayne	107
THE BOUNCE OF LIFE	About the one and only Earl the Pearl, a friend, a superb athlete, and a one of a kind real human being	131
THE CROWN OF SCIENCE	To scientist Albert Einstein	198
THE CURE	The curing of disease of all kinds	319
THE DEFEATED	To be number one-- but there is number two-- defeated is that so?	350
THE DISEASE, THAT IS SILENT!	Poem dedicated to the American Diabetes Association-- Community Service Award Dinner	408
THE END AND THE BEGINNING	The ways of life	390
THE GROUP OF SIX	To my friends and clients, the Optical House, Dick Swanek, Irwin Schmizer, Sandy Duke, Dick Rauh, Richard Rowholt and Willi Tomas	216

THE GUILT OF A SOLDIER	To Lt. Callay, Soldier-- Vietnam War	237
THE LOSS OF A LOVE	Love-- the asking for it	316
THE LUST FOR WAR	What war does and what it could be--	306
THE MAN	A man-- we all love and admire Jackie Mason-- the entertainer	268
THE MEETING OF STRANGERS	The looking for a woman and hoping	294
THE NEIGHBORHOOD	Thanks to the Bronx, Creston JHS 79 and club and friends "The Flicks"	151
THE PICTURE OF LIFE	What one accomplishes in life	244
THE REMEMBERANCE OF A POET	A poet who died in Greenwich Viillage	332
THERE'S A LOT TO SEE	Look to God and see afar-- there's much to see and love and have	219
THE REST OF YOUR LIFE	Taking all for granted	94
THE ROUND TABLE OF PEACE	Peace conferences of the world	306
THE SEA OF GRASS	Tall grass swaying-- it looked to me	374
THE SHADOW HAS PASSED	Former President Nixon-- when shadows appeared for him	291
THE SILENCE OF THE DIAMOND	To the late Gil Hodges of the Brooklyn Dodgers and Manager of the New York Mets, who helped me catch in 1948	147
THE STRENGTH OF TEARS	To Wendy, my daughter, my love, and me-- her heart exploration	43
THE TIME OF YOUR LIFE	To find out that life is there!	259
THE TIME OF YOUR LIFE	For anyone whose time is now	296
THE TIME WILL COME	Thoughts of time passing only to know we shall meet	301
THE TIN CAN	That which we all use, love, disrespect and take for granted	233
THE TRUE MEANING	The meaning of a friend-- coming to Rome Italy-- from Miami, Hawaii when learning of me being sick-- Shep Gordon	159
THE UNFAIRNESS OF DEATH	To a friend, my late dentist	189

THE WORST HAS PASSED	When somebody dies and the strength one must have	345
TILL LOVE	Love-- what it is	211
TILL NEXT WE MEET	The meeting of friends once again	319
TILL SOON	The family and what it is to all of us	263
TIME	The passing of "Time"	292
TIME BETWEEN FRIENDS	To Alan Grubman and Arthur Indursky	158
TO ASK FOR LOVE	To ask and want of love	322
TO BE AFRAID	The feeling of being afraid	171
TO BE A JEW	To be Jewish	241
TO BE REAL	To be real to yourself	397
TO CRY	The feeling to cry and its relief	198
TO DREAM- THE IMPOSSIBLE DREAM	The dreams of us all to have	195
TODAY IS ELLEN	To my beloved daughter Ellen	41
TO END ONE'S LIFE	To the late Susan Hayward--	48
TO GIVE ONESELF	One should always give oneself in life	43
TO GOD	An ill Japanese woman in the hospital bed next to mine in Rome, Italy	227
TO HATE	What hate is and why?	257
TO HAVE LOVED, THEN NOT AT ALL	To hope for love-- then not to have it at all	349
TO LEAVE A HOUSE OF LOVE	What it would mean to leave my home	356
TO LOSE ONES LOVE	Another captures your love	375
TO LOVE	Love-- with each other	272
TOMORROW	Live today not for tomorrow	191
TOO TIRED TO SLEEP	Trying to fall asleep,	256
TO SAY GOODBYE	When saying goodbye	382

TO SPEAK THE TRUTH	A trilogy-- a story of life between a father, a mother, a son in Nazi Germany	175
TO THE ARMS OF MY WORK	Thank you, to the people that helped me in my work and profession	287
TRUE INNOCENCE	The feeling of innocence	386
TRY TO REMEMBER	Remember what has happened	192
TURTLES OF MUSIC	To my friends and clients of the Mix Place-- John Quinn, Bobby Elder, Ken Frederickson, Charles Wick	86
TWO BOYS	Two of the warmest, sincerest, human beings one can find in one's lifetime-- Armand Braiger and Mario DeMartini, owners and proprietors of New York City's best restaurant, One if By Land, Two if By Sea	154
TWO TO COME	A summer romance to continue?	312
UNFORGETTABLE	To my late friend and God Father to my daughter Ellen, an actor Montgomery Clift	45
UNFORGOTTEN DEATH	Death, suddenly happening and to be with us forever	332
WATER THE FLOWERS	Aspects of life and what it's really about	209
WEARING A MASK	An impression of the coach of George Washington University. His thoughts of blacks and the chance of opportunity	400
WHAT A CROWD	A crowd captured by - THE CARS	221
WHAT DO I WANT?	What people want of love	330
WHAT I ASK OF YOU	What men need of women	279
WHAT I HEARD	Listening to a rock concert	344
WHAT IS A CARD	What a greeting card is to me,	247
WHAT IS A WOMAN?	Women, and what it is a man	243
WHAT IS IT ALL ABOUT?	Life-- what is it??	243
WHAT IS WOMAN	Woman, how wonderful	243
WHAT I WANT	What a person wants	250
WHAT MAKES HIM MY SON?	To my son, Scott	202
WHEN WE GROW UP	Christmas-- we all tend not to grow up	294

WHERE AM I	What? and where am I to life	179
WHERE AM I NOW	I am here now because of Bobby	158
WHO AM I?	How a black man feels-- no different than a white man	234
WHO IS ALEX?	In memory of Alex Sadkin-- music producer for Duran Duran, Thompson Twins, Simply Red, Talking Heads, Robbie Neville	384
WHY CAST THE FIRST STONE	To former President Nixon and what the Bible says	143
WHY DID IT HAPPEN	Life-- and why things happen	253
WHY NOT?	To dream of your dreams	292
WITH YOU	Doing together with someone you love	372
WORDS HAVE TOO MANY SHADOWS	When one talks, the words have shadows, doubts, etc.	94
WORDS I COULD NOT EXPRESS	Feelings that couldn't be expressed in words only	29
XMAS, IS A FRAME OF MIND?	Xmas, should be all year round.	394
YEARS TOGETHER	My years together with Bobby, my wife	357
YES, I LOVE YOU	To my mother-in-law, Sylvia and - father-in-law, Jerry Thomases	61
YES OR NO	The choice to live	176
YESTERDAY'S DAY	Wanting yesterday to last forever	340
YOU	To a client and friend, Luther Vandross	121
YOU ARE YOUR OWN	A woman's desire to succeed	302
YOU MY FRIEND	To Gary Kurfirst-- many years together	221
YOUR CHANCE SHALL COME	Hoping that one's desire will come	320
YOUTH IS WASTED ON THE YOUNG	A reflection I've come to as I see various aspects of my life before me	229
YOUR NEW LIFE	A new life for two	362
YOU'VE JUST BEGUN	To Ann Ronson Jones, Mick Jones and their new son	66

THE YANKEES

INVITE *Pastell*

1950 VICTORY DINNER
8:00 P.M.

BILTMORE HOTEL
Ballroom — 19th Floor

Bowman Team

PERSONAL USE ONLY

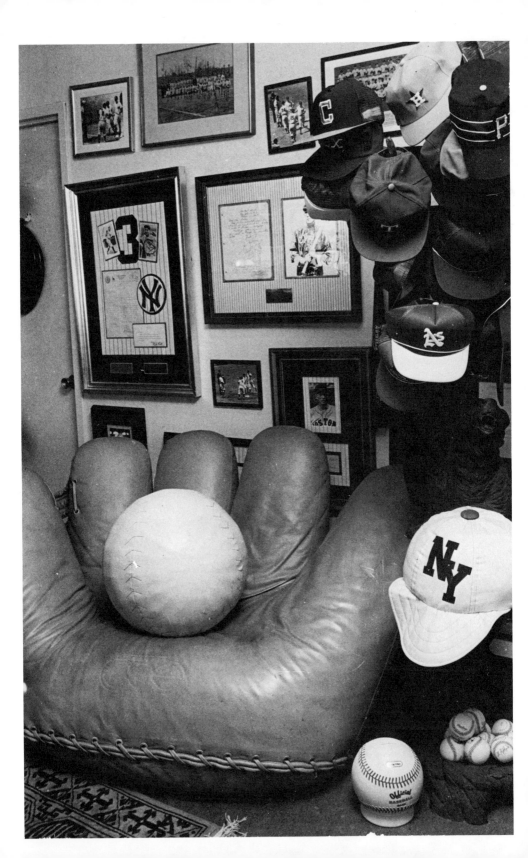

From Joe DiMaggio:

      During my thirteen year career with the New York Yankees, Bert Padell was the greatest batboy I ever saw. He was with us for two years (1949-1950) and was the most enthusiastic hustler the Yankees ever had. He had a fine right arm, and caught batting practice- handling such pitchers as Vic Raschi, Allie Reynolds, Ed Lopat, Joe Page, and Whitey Ford. More than thirty years have passed since then and Bert continues to excell. He handles all my affairs and business transactions, and looks after my career as though it were his own. In both baseball and business, Bert Padell has exhibited a sure eye, a steady hand, and can still tell the difference between a curve or a sinker whether it comes from the pitching mound or the stock market.

Joe DiMaggio

ENJOY!

We must never accept
either in thought or deed
what we have.
Accept it,
Strive for better, if your
inner feelings desire so.
Strive for it!
But, most of all, enjoy
    the fruits of life.

Enjoy God's word
His song of love and desire,
    for His love for one's fellow man
Yet most, enjoy oneself.
There is no better than God's creation.

Enjoy love and desire what
Your man or woman give you
not for their beauty or luscious body
but for them
alone

Their smile as it delights
your eyes and body.
Their talk and desire
    to be with or work with
Their dress and being with you
    as your King or Queen
As well as enjoy your desires
    with them.
Your body tingling with each
    kiss and love touch.

Life is one challenge
The rhapsody of life
Is your fulfillment of every day
    as much as you can of life
Change it, because it is a story,
To some short, while to the fortunate
    it becomes a novel
To each its own
But to each one's enjoyment fulfilled
    Enjoy life and you.

A SONG OF LIFE

I shall never want
I shall never need
A song
A verse
So long as I have you

The song of life
Is the staff of being
Each word a sparkle and
Meaning of you.
The sound and echoes are of life
With you
My dear, my love
My song of life

Never a challenge to young and old
Always a partner to all
The song of life
Is within us all
It is our love and desire
For each other,
It's music never ending.

SING TO YOURSELF

Each morning of my life
I hear the echoes of the day
Will I create
Or will they conquer
Those—out there—
The knaves
My heart fills with love
I sing to myself
To be heard by all
But especially you, love of my life
You make it easier
   to wake up
   to desire
   to live
For you are my song
To hear the echoes of
   the mountain
The drops of water
   on one's heart.
I shall overcome
And sing not only to myself
But, to all loud and clear
The day will be fresh
   for you and me.

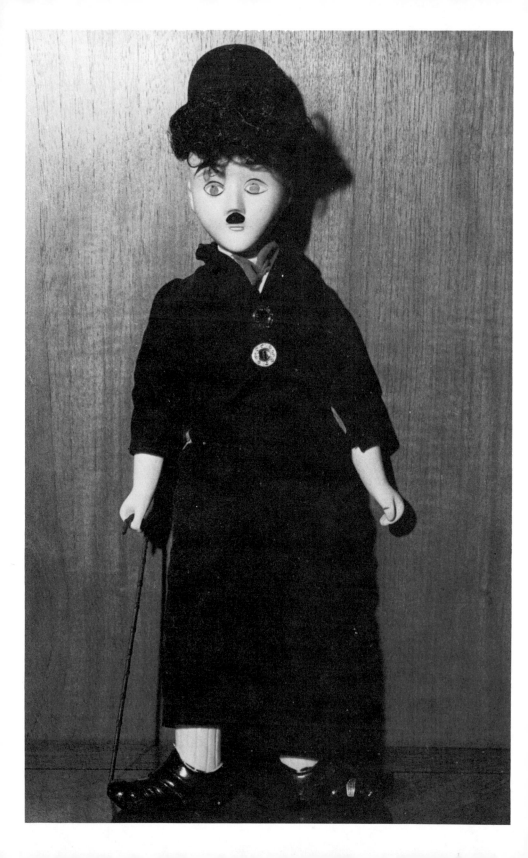

WORDS I COULD NOT EXPRESS

The seasons of our life
express many feelings and moods.
The springs of summer create
a waiting feeling.
The winds of winter create
an icy chill.
With these experiences I am never
hungry for thought or talk.

Yet, when we met for the first time
everything was still.
You were exactly what my mind pictured.
You create the flowers of life.
Your every movement is a rhapsody.

Yes, we are strangers,
But only in distance.
When you speak
Your voice echoes from within.
The knaves of my world dissipate
when your energies emerge
from the stage.

I am truly sorry
that this was not said
to you directly,
your wit, your talent
are God's gift to you.
Now there is one beside you,
always loving you,
knowing that the rainbow will glow
from the riches you give to all.

To my beloved wife and friend, Bobby.

SO YOUNG

Her smile warms my feelings,
Its pleasant ever-lasting strength, not meek or bleak
But captivating for all those who expose themselves to her.
Not tall or short
Yet firm buoyant is she.
Your eye would sure to catch her,
Any day of the year.
Her carefree desires of life
She does walk with—
Unafraid.
Unknowing, what they may be.
An astute thought she has, conquering your heart.
Her years to very young.
The seed of life she has not fully tasted.
God's wonders are strange; yet very distant to her.
Youth is just a word, its meaning has been fulfilled to her.
My thoughts, desires, and hopes,
She has become a partner to.
Her fickle ways make life so puzzling,
To show all my earthly cares for her.
Yet as time moves, it never waits for anybody.
Her thoughts shall be mine.
And my life hers.
Then, "So Young" she shall not be.
Tis true, I have found my life sinew.

HOW MUCH CAN ONE TAKE?

This life with all its
   hills and slopes

Men and women try to
   succeed

The evils of war
The horrors of pain

Yet, we all know
   too well

That we ourselves
   bring them forth

Not to be gentle
Or sane
But careless
Inhuman
   to ourselves

Our bodies
Our very beings

We ask ourselves
What makes such
   a being
Do such things

The answer, we're human

And that is the reason
   for error

Yet, the flower of beauty
   is life

In every capacity of
   life's venture

Its den of comfort
Its horror of self-destruction

Its beauty beyond a dream

On the ways it could be

Yet how little it takes
   for self-destruction

One must say,
   we shall overcome
   all evil and hardship

Live for today
For tomorrow will come

What may be, will be

Try to respect
   and love all things
   and beings

And, best of all,
   love thyself from within

The pressures of life and
   the firmament of God's will and love

We can take what will come
Hoping all will be great love and enchantment.

SENSITIVITY

This is not for just a day
but for a lifetime
It is how one feels
each moment
each thought
each hour of one's life
For without this
there is no life
no happening
no nearness
no wanting
no caring

With this God's gift
You are life
All should have it
treasure it
nurture it
Its absence
is like a mountain without snowcaps
Is like fields of fresh cut grass
without a scent
Like love without you
Love embracing without the tingle and
moment of rapture
To have you cry
and laugh
Within the span of a minute

All that is the luxury of life
All that gives one
A sense of life
The intangible of sensitivity

To Faye Dunaway, my friend and client.

A LADY CHASING THE WIND

Her voice soft and low
Distinct and clear
Her eyes soft as a baby's kiss
Her love warm to some she loves
Yet, this charming woman of women
Is always chasing the wind
Never able to catch or feel its breath.

She has so much
But feels she has so little
Her love is burning yet she
Fears to let it bubble over
Why, oh why
Do so many love her?

Her life, oh so busy,
Like a top spinning from
One place to another
Yet, one must slow down
Or, a headache will destroy
One's self

Her loved ones always have
Their hands out to her
Please, touch them.
They do love you,
Caress them, or the wind will
Blow them away.
Love and respect are words.
They respect you and your work
But you must give of yourself.

For one can live only once.
And cherish the freshness
Of the snow on one's face
Like that of love, for the wind
Has stopped
And awaits you and your love.

Music by John Fetter
Lyrics by John Fetter +
    Gail Simon +
    Bert Padell

LADY CHASING THE WIND

Calligraphy by Kevin Misevis

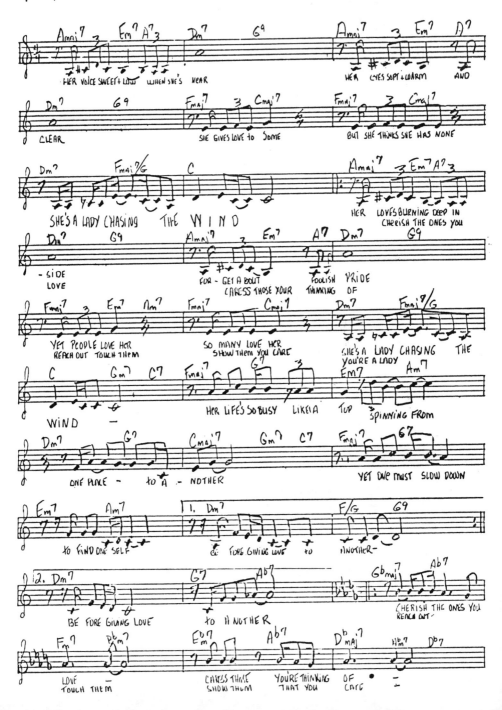

LADY CHASING THE WIND

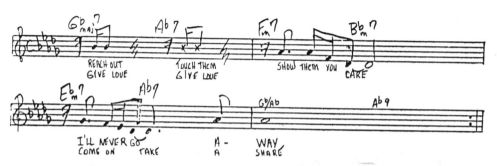

REACH OUT / GIVE LOVE — TOUCH THEM / GIVE LOVE — SHOW THEM YOU CARE

I'LL NEVER GO / COME ON — TAKE — A- / A — WAY / SHARE

Dearest Bert,

You are an extraordinary man, whose cup of
kindness is always overflowing. If I had one
wish it would be to give you all that you have
given to others.

All my love always,

Faye Dunaway

To a former client and friend, Ali McGraw,
when she was a fashion model.

A GIRL CALLED ALI

This day like yesterday
      or
Yesterday's yesterday
but different.
The sun rose with its little
nose peeking through the dawn,
Its color gleaming

The sky pale,
Yet the bluest of seas
The air fresh and sweet
like that of the nightingale
Today is here
Such a good day.

I see
a
tall slim frame
tall, yet not too. Strong as a tree in the wind,
Swaying with each gust.

As fresh, after a hard dismal rain,
As sweet as fresh cut roses
As everlasting as perfume
As shocking as mini mini
As charming as a first date
As appealing as a tight skirt
As wanting as a first kiss
As loving as a quiet smile

This was Ali

Is this a dream?
Yet dubious thoughts
      come to pass
my eyes saw
my nose captured the aroma
my taste conquered
my heart whistled
my mind was contained
that such a girl called Ali should
      appear.

To my beloved daughter Ellen.

TODAY IS ELLEN

Each day I look at her
And try to remember
How little she was—
My little girl and oh so little

As the years did pass
My little girl stopped
Being little
Yet, always my little girl.

Today I see her
Tall, with sweetness of a sugar stick
Her thoughts hers,
Which I cherish.
When right I hope she
Stands straight for it;
When in doubt or wrong, oh please,
May she sway like a beautiful tree in the wind
Never to crack in the storm
Because of changing with the time
Her figure like that of a goddess
Tall and slick and tender
Ever caressing

Each year that passes
She will change,
Grow into womanhood
and then some day
Leave for a further life,
A greater feeling and wanting.
But, she will always be
Part of me—
My heart
My soul
My being
For she is my Ellen of today and
    Always

*To Wendy—my daughter and love—
her heart exploration.*

THE STRENGTH OF TEARS

Each of us holds our own destiny
Each of us shares our own love
Each of us shares despair and depression
Yet few of us share one special treasure
To shed a tear is a sign of strength
It shows a heart within
A longing to be a part of something
A need
A wanting
To belong
But especially to care
The strength of the heart is the staff of life,
The tears of joy and tears of sorrow
For they show we are human
And care for life and man.

TO GIVE ONESELF

Always in my life
I've strived for love and fairness to all
For each of us has a day of reckoning.
We might fear that day
Yet the beauty of life is beyond a dream.

Each time we give ourselves to someone
Hurt, deceit, disappointment can occur.
For there are some who are animals of the jungle
living off whatever suits them.
Their day will come
They will be alone in the forest
With no sound,
No songs of the birds
And no light of life

One should not despair
One must give oneself at all moments
For that is the joy and love of life.

A Definition of Friendship

"Friendship is the comfort, the inexpressible comfort of feeling safe with a person having neither to weigh thoughts nor measure words, but pouring all right out just as they are, chaff and grain together, certain that a faithful friendly hand will take and sift them, keep what is worth keeping and with a breath of comfort, blow the rest away."

To my late friend and actor—
Montgomery Clift.

UNFORGETTABLE

Many times in my life I've tried to forget
things, places, people.
There were times when I accomplished this feat,
But you my friend are unforgettable as years pass.
Thru life's day many happenings occur
Sudden—fast—
Only to be forgotten the next day,
But your friendship is unforgettable.
Each day that passes I earn my living
To some it is a week's vacation, to others a rich man's delight.
Your fortune never curtails our friendship.
Money can only be spent, while friendship never can be bought.
There are many luxuries by my side
All of them at my command
King I am to them
Yet a slave if your friendship I could not find.
Fortunate I am to be loved
Without this love, life would be empty,
Few I love very dearly,
You my friend are a part of this love.
My friend, you can talk with kings and never lose your carefree
    manner
Each banner of accomplishment you do achieve,
Never sways your mind because of stardom.
The finest tribute to man itself, is you.
There are many astute men of our time
Their feats never to be forgotten
Yet if our friendship should pass with time
It would be death itself.

Personal feelings—
Jackie Jensen and Montgomery Clift
during the filming of The Misfits.

Upper Left: The beautiful Truckee River which bisects the city and the famous Virginia Street Bridge.
Lower Left: Virginia Street — Hub of the 24 hour gambling excitement — Reno Arch in background.
Right Vertical: World famous Harold's Club — seven stories devoted to the best in gambling, fine food and entertainment.

P24575

AIR MAIL

Dear Bert

Have finally met our friend Montgomery Clift. We wish you were here to enjoy Reno with us. Quite a coincidence, but he is just as you described. Jackie

How about such a coincidence! Th right — what a nice guy — Love to you 3 — Mort —

POST CARD

Mr. & Mrs. Bert Radell
34 - 41   78th St.
Jackson Heights 72
New York

AIR MAIL

Plastichrome by COLOURPICTURE PUBLISHERS, INC., Boston 15, Mass., U.S.A.
Reno News Agency — Reno, Nevada

Color by Mac Miller

CRYSTAL BAY
AUG 3 PM 1960 NEV.

From Jackie Jensen—
All-American Football Player,
American League Baseball Star
and my deceased best friend.

To whom it may concern:

Once, long ago, I thought I could help teach Bert about life, family and friendship. Now he is the teacher and I the learner.

He makes friendship a warm, living and unforgettable delight. To best describe his poems, I quote Bert himself, "One cannot forget words from the heart."

A friend, Jackie Jensen

TO END ONE'S LIFE

Your time on earth has almost come to an end
Beauty and glory have come your way
Love has been a stranger to you
Fear not, my lady, many do love thee.

To end your life before your time has come,
    one cannot believe
As beauty like yours seen in the firmament of God.

May your chance for life touch your heart:

There will be mourning, if your life goes to
    dust.

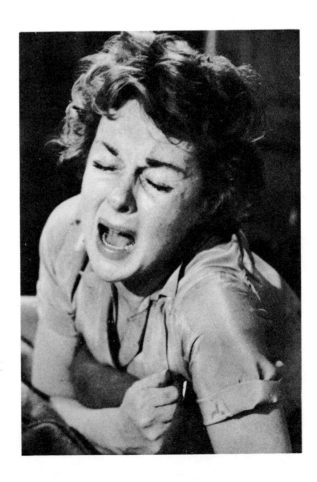

Dear Mr. Padell,

Thank you so much for your thoughtfulness
in writing to me, and for the lovely poem.

Your interest is deeply appreciated, and
may I wish you everything that makes life
wonderful?

Most sincerely,

Susan Hayward

Dear Bert, Please give these two a job ok...at least a bus ticket home—XXX

MAKING TRACKS
THE RISE OF BLONDIE
BY DEBBIE HARRY, CHRIS STEIN, AND VICTOR BOCKRIS

To Debbie Harry—Blondie

DEBORAH

This field of entertainment
Moods that the world uses
To satisfy a need for relaxing.
It is part of our life
A need of our diet
And a must for a special group.

In our lifetime
there appeared
a petite white skinned woman,
And what a Woman!!!
Her hair at times like straw
and rainbow colored.
When dressed up,
It would shine
Reminiscent of gold.

Her voice pleasant
and easy listening to
Her words from the music she
shares with guys like "what's happening,"
who share her life.

Other members of the band
Strengthened by the words
and tones that come from her voice.
All can talk with her
She is strong as a Joan of Arc
She is gentle as a Venus
She is a gem to the world
She is Debbie to us all!!!

This lady of the world
Dresses to her liking
Never looking back
to question the result.

She and her group BLONDIE,
her five loveable guys
create and give music to our lives.
Asking only one thing in return—
Enjoy and forget the troubles of life
Listen to their music
and dream your dreams away.

From Debbie Harry of
Blondie

Bert Padell writes poetry
To stop the hands of time.
And make complete his wild-
est thoughts
And never miss a beat.

XX All my love
Debbie Harry

From Fran Lebowitz—
Famous writer (Metropolitan Life,
Social Studies)

Dear Bert,

I should like to take this opportunity to point out that although I admire and respect you with unbridled passion I am not entirely happy to be confronted with someone so riddled with talent the he is able not only to read contracts, but also to write books.

Your friend,
Fran Lebowitz

BUT FOR LOVE

I feel many wants of life
The desire of your hand next to mine
caressing each whimper of my body
to this desire is one fruitful need
of mine and all
Yet, the deepest of man and
    woman
is love.

Love is the beauty of your
    thoughts to mine
Love is your tears caressing
    your cheek to mine
Love is forgiving me when I am
    nasty and cruel,
moody and shy
Love is the freshness of your smile
Like that of the flower bud.

Love is a song of movements,
its lyric caressing, feeling of each other,
Yet the fullest desire of life
is love itself.
For, without it
there is no life
or wanting of life.

It creates all
desires all
and makes life
worth living.

SWEETNESS OF MY LOVES

Quiet as a morning sea
Still as a breezeless day
My thoughts wonder!
The sweetness of my loves

My second love is
Sweet
Loving
Daring
Wanting love in return
Her carelessness to be loved
Astute or wanting
The movements of her body
Striking
As a wave caresses another on a calm sunny day.
She is my second love.

My third love is
Quiet
Unsure
Loving
Wanting
Hurting
Closeness to him
For he carries my name and my picture on his face
He hurts few, but many knaves pursue him
Only to be strong as granite
Times, unsure of people—
of knowing
of love
He is my third love.

My fourth love is
Spoiled
Loving
Captivating
Her years but one
She has given much to life
A sister to her brother
A friend to her sister,
A bundle of love to her nannies
Careless but swift love to many
Made life a little sweeter to her mom
Made a king of her daddy.

Yet how little it takes
 for self-destruction

One must say,
 we shall overcome
 all evil and hardship

Live for today
For tomorrow will come

What may be, will be

Try to respect
 and love all things
 and beings

And, best of all,
 love thyself from within

The pressures of life and
 the firmament of God's will and love

We can take what will come
Hoping all will be great love and enchantment.

ERNIE CATANESE AND BERT PADELL

To Ernie Catanese, my friend—
He is The Friend.

MY DESIRE

Time passes ever so quickly
A stranger to none,
With a shadow of hope
For one to find a friend.
A friend to some,
Will be a foe to others.
The warmth of his presence,
Will be frigid to others.
Let man have all the riches of the universe
Let man have all the careless desires of life.
What I wish,
Where is this friend?

A FRIENDSHIP

Time has made our friendship,
from childhood to manhood.
Your ways of love similar to mine,
but the years have projected us apart.
The force of a greater love you do seek.
My friend, I do fear we are drifting apart.

AN EMPTY FEELING

This day hurt has unfolded.
My friend's father, strong and illustrious,
Has died.
Why?
So young was he.
His son, will he grieve?
I wonder!
As his friend
I think he would be bereft in losing a father.
The word in itself has a sinew sincerity.
The calmness of a stream in summer,
Was his characterization of life.
A stentorian voice was his, but soft in its meaning...
I know my friend will miss him,
As love for each other was innate within them,
And now an emptiness.

REMEMBER OUR LOVE

Remember each fragrance
Each flower petal
Ever hoping
To draw to life
And open our hearts
to know and have
gentle love
Betrayal never happening
The ghosts of loneliness
Are mere shadows
Ah, sweet time of love
Our love
Like that of children laughing
This love
Never touched with despair
Alive and strong
Without fear or toil
This verse of true love
Ours.

REMEMBER WHAT I DID

Remember me a little
The business of day to day
I did create,
The worries that troubled you
I did conquer
to still your pain.

Sing out to all
The names you feared
For now and evermore
their sound is silence.

All are but a memory
A dream
A bad dream
But never an empty day again.

All this I ask you
to remember
To remember what I did
Let it not be in vain.

YES, I LOVE YOU

Each hour of the day
my thoughts hunger for you
to know that you are there
waiting, desiring only me
Oh, just a feeling
Yes, I do love you.

I love you to the end of eternity
Until the earth falls off into space
Until man never desires woman
Until the sky changes from blue to yellow
Until God takes me from you.

Oh, what a joyful life I have with you
I need you
and want you
I only hope your feelings are the same.
Yes, I love you, only you.

My darling, dear, beloved
Your soft voice and body are
my desire
Your nearness is my only comfort
Your being intertwines with mine
Your are my life, my meaning
    for you make me complete.
Oh, yes, I do love you.

To my friend Ben Vereen.

BEN
(The Root of a Man)

He first came to us
From a small speck on the map.
He was unknown.
His breeches were worn; his roots were firm
He was of middle frame
with dark skin and bright teeth.
His eyes were soft
And endearing to the soul
His voice was low
But with the sparkle of something special,
There for his mark on life.

He felt a kinship
to dance and song
That was his spot, his creation,
his knowing
and belonging.
When he entertained,
the art of life was created
The songs of life
We remember from where we came

His roots sparkling with life
Showering upon us
Making us enjoy him.
Sometimes laughing
For he is man
A person of being
A person of love
A person of affection
This man soft and gentle

The wealth of his act
Is from his roots of fortune
The desire to succeed
is seen in his eyes and smile
The audience is his food
His drink is their applause
His accomplishment is finding
   and knowing his roots,
And the man that he is.

BEN

To Bert-

How does one find words to say how
wonderful you are, or how much you
mean to me and my family, as God knows.
And I personally, along with my
family, say "Oh what a wonder you
are. When we were down you picked us
up."

Love always
Chicken Vee
(Ben)

*To Ann Ronson, Mick Jones
and their new son—*

YOU'VE JUST BEGUN

All through our lives
We strive
hard and fast
Some to achieve the impossible,
Others the heights of the foreseen
through this path of do's and don'ts

The scars of life appear on our bodies
The wise ones care for each one
healing one by one
While many try
and scramble to avoid them completely
only to have the blood of life
remain throughout life.

You, my friend, must be wise
and keep a fresh clear mind
You are young
not in years perhaps
but in living life's ways.
Looking at you is soft endearing to the eyes
Your voice is gentle and cooling to the soul
You have God's gift, which few are fortunate to have,
A child of your choice

Your face a mirror to hers
Your warmth
Your love
Your caressing
Yet, best of all your endearing love
with all its sweetness
for her and with your love
you have to be ready and willing to give.
The lips upon your face
gentle with talk
Hungry for the touch of that extra someone
other than your little one.

All this you have
and more, waiting and ready,
Your life has only begun
For your child
For yourself
and for that one who is a speck on the horizon
For you shall make unto your strength of life
and dearest love of love
you are very special to yourself and others
and then, only then,
Your life will have just begun.

FOREIGNER

An honor's degree in life's
university,
A man you can count on
in times of adversity,
A head full of numbers, eight
days every week,
But the mind of an artist,
and a heart that can speak,
So refreshing to find, that this
business man,
Is a rare human being, yes
'Bert' understands,

Mick Jones.

From David Byrne of the Talking Heads

Bert always, and I mean always,
asks how I'm doin'
and take care...(a serious reminder),
What d'ya think? Huh?
What's he eat for breakfast?
I hear he works long hours.
He lives within walking distance of me.
Well listen buddy, I work long hours too..
My work don't stop at the office
But I can call him at home, so I guess
his doesn't either.
When I was younger, the concept of an
accountant did not enter my mind, and
an accountant who wrote poetry was not
within the realm of possibilities.
WELL NOT ANY MORE.

68

From Tina—
of the Talking Heads music group

DEAR BERT.

THANK YOU VERY MUCH FOR ALL YOUR CARING - YOU'VE BEEN A REAL FRIEND. FROM A PURELY SELFISH POINT OF VIEW, I HOPE YOU OUTLIVE ME, 'CAUSE I SURE CAN'T DO WITHOUT YOU - NOR CHRIS, NOR ROBIN.

LOVE,

Tina

THE AWARD

As they announce who has won
You all wonder
Is it I, is it they.
To be there is enough
For so few are ever here
Your heart
Your speech
   are at 78 speed.
   on a 33⅓ turntable.

It will be over
But for you it has just begun
For today was a loss
But it is the beginning of your tomorrows.

From Ric Ocasek—
of the Cars

Dear Bert,

    there you are
    atop the chunky churches
    atop the square lit windows
    atop the clocks
    ticking tock
    there you are
    between lost and found
    and modern sound
    diving into the wreck
    and emerging
    with a hope for happiness

        Love,
        Ric Ocasek

LOOK OF LOVE

His body's rhythm
Embraced the room
Reflected his soul
Creating each movement of arms and legs
Caressing the air with music.

Oh, such a beat
Piercing your eyes
Rhapsodic moments enhancing the beat.

The look of love
will last forever,
As long as ever can be.

Letter from Bonnie Pointer

To Bert

Many come but only few stay!
You will be one of the
few lifelong friends in
my world

But do me a favor

Don't try to sing

And I won't write a book

Bonnie
Pointer

To a music manager, Dee Anthony.

OUR MAN DEE

Each sound beats through us all.
We feel each chord and note
Expressing a thought to us.

It is our life
Our destiny
Our love
Our Man Dee made this possible

Music is with us each day.
It expresses love, sorrow, joy and
    tear drop stories.
With each breath, it creates a feeling
    Of Drama
    Of Love
    Of Rock
    Of Life.
For with music it creates
A story to be told
And how one unfolds it.
This our Man Dee made possible.
Who? This man Dee!
May he be
An image
A name
A story
A soul
No!!!
He created us,

Put us together,
Molded, fit and dressed us
to be what we are today,
    Our Man Dee.
Yet, when all despaired
He kept up
Never once a frown
Always, my boys, the top!
None better,
No seconds

He was our only salvation
To know what to do
At the right time
And knowing when the right time was.
   Our Man Dee

What is he?
Our Manager
Our storybook father.
In need he is with us
In joy he joins us.
In sorrow his hand touches ours.
Our Partner
Our love
   Our Man Dee
How do we thank him
Caress him
Love Him

Our guide to our career
Our guide to our life!
Each one of us
Can only say
In a whisper
   Our Man Dee,
We Do Love thee
   And
      Thank thee.

To friends, and stars in their own way—
Alice Cooper and Shep Gordon

ALICE AND SHEP

One should ask
have you found the perfect partner,
Not in image
but in the cruel, cold world
   of business?
I have seen two men
that God has touched to be one,
Alice and Shep.

Each one has molded
   each for each other.
They each bow to and create
   for each other.
Where one lacks, the other
   shines.
Where one is shy, the other
   is steady and strong
Alice and Shep.

What is Alice?
He is quiet, with friends
wanting to be part of his bunch.
Fun to talk with
Ever hoping for you to listen to his talk.
Sportsman in his wanting,
the tee and the bat are his
   sword.
How does one speak of
such a gentle creature?

A word is not enough
for his sincerity and ever loving desire
   to be part of your inner thoughts.
There should be a place in the City
   for such as he
For there are too few of him.
Oh, such man has God created
   of which we all share such a small
   piece.

His partner, Shep, is a man of men.
There is none better than he,
No warmth or ties stronger
   to this man Alice.
He is the creator,
The genius
The royalist as if he were King.

Errors and omissions occur
Yet he is ready, able to grasp another
   from them.

Through criticism he learns
With his astute, captivating mind
He is a manager of talent.
A friend like precious jewels.
A partner like that of a lover.
He walks with the wind
And never loses his common touch.
This man Shep.

I look in the window.
Looking in
the glass is weeping
for the desire to say
Fortunate I am,
Gifted to know
Two gentle
Two astute
Two human beings
Who sprinkled life's joys.
What all men seek
I have found,
In Alice and Shep.

Dear Bert,

I have tried for a month to write a
letter for your book, unsuccessfully.

Somehow words aren't good enough to
describe Bert Padell, truly a man made
in the image of God. I can only hope
for anyone reading this book you can
meet one man throughout your life that
is half the man of Bert, a man for whom
the word friend was made.

Your friend & admirer,

Shep

From Alice Cooper

After much study, calculating and
advanced math techniques we have
computed that you, Bert Padell, are
the highest source of natural energy
on this planet.

I was asked if I could ask you to
donate your body to the govt. so as
to run off the energy of your personal
self. I mean all the business and the
poetry too! It would only be for a
year or two, until this oil thing is
settled.

All we would have to do is find a way
to connect you, in some way, to all the
generators in the U.S. We could possibly
run all the wires into one wire and
stick it in you somewhere.

Thank you for all your effort in Shep's
and my behalf and for your patriotism.

Your friend and confidante,

P.S. We will dub it
"Padellucian Power"

Rarely, in my experiences, do you run into a successful "businessman" who also has the heart and soul of an "artist", but when I met Bert Padell, I knew I had found the exception to the rule. Not only does he expertly handle the careers of many of today's Superstars, he genuinely feels and expresses encouragement to his people on a gut level that is crucial and deeply appreciated by all of us "crazies". To be honest, I wouldn't put up with or be able to handle half of the frustrations he must endure daily to help all of us "keep it together" in this wild world of entertainment.

After reading "Bert's Words", his first book of poetry, I knew I'd found a new friend and fellow poet; one who's very bottom line is the joy found in expressing his feelings for the people in his life in words, to me, the greatest gift of all.

Thanks again Bert, and I know you'll touch many a heart with your newest collection. You all are in for a very special treat !

Even Stevens

To James Malloy and David Malloy and Even Stevens,
father, son & friend—producers and songwriters together.

A FATHER, A SON, A FRIEND.

One could travel the world
to find people
warm in heart
high in ideals
and open in love.

It did happen
in music country
Where music is a way of life
Its every meaning is the fabric of being
and existing.
In this little house of their's
There were three,
A Father, a Son, a Friend.
They are all in love with life
And all its beauties
Free from the bottomless pits of
dark thoughts
Free and true to whomever they encounter
Their bonanza comes from music and words
The sensitivity of each from their lives
A Father, a Son, a Friend.
A father who is a friend to his son
A son who loves his dad as a father
and as a caring friend.
A friend who has found friends in this
Father and Son.
Searching and appearing as part
of his day
The three feathers
Walking in the sun and never shading their eyes
No fear of the dark
For their path is written in time
For love and peace
They have found within
The Father, the Son, the Friend.

To my friend the truck driver.

THE BACK END

His face was calm
The body didn't wiggle or twist,
At ease with the world as he backed in his huge ton truck.
He never did ask for help.
Traffic did stop, for hours it did seem.
Many other cars had their angry look of patience,
He never had a doubtful feeling on his face
Full of confidence and courage, for a task he
    had done many times awaited him.
Swiftly turning the wheel,
Little beads of sweat appear on his forehead
His heart beats slightly faster than usual.
At ease with the world he feels
The space is small and only a master can conquer.
Traffic and noise are his only audience;
Another turn of the wheel and slowly the back-end.

I PRAY TO GOD

The night is still and dark,
A cold breeze I do feel in my body.
At this time I feel in an indolent state of being
The sounds of life my ears cannot prevail.
Want of prayer, I do seek.
Does one such as I pray?
But all one can do is pray, and hope he will be heard.
A stentorian voice I do not have; but hope to be heard,
    I pray.
I pray to God to forgive all bad,
I pray to ask him to welcome all to his sight
To have all turn and shake the hand of his enemy.
This I ask to you my father of being.
As I pray the night air is warm and clear,
The stars sparkle upon my face,
The feeling of God's presence
Tis true, he has heard my prayer.

To Stephanie Mills, my friend

I STEPHANIE

The crowd was waiting
expecting
with patience
and anticipation
that their gal was coming
to entertain
excite
and engross them in pleasure.

It happened
The one and only
I Stephanie
captured the audience
tantalizing them
hypnotizing them

She has arrived
She has come down from the road
through the rain
through the storm
arriving with song
and love,
touching us
warming our hearts with light dreams of love.

The voice, the gift of God
From her mother and father who guided her
to fame
Her sisters and brothers who brought the
foundation of life to her.
To find her companion in life
who enjoys and shares her fame.

This little lady
brings to us
fulfillment and love
and makes us move
with the silken chords of her voice.

She is I Stephanie
there is no one of voice and
movement on stage to help us
all remember
what talent and warmth is only from Stephanie—

To my friends and clients of the Mix Place—
John Quinn, Bobby Elder, Charles Wick,
Ken Frederickson.

TURTLES OF MUSIC

My first impression of them was quiet
Unassuming, gentle
With each passing week
A tie intercoursed us together
As I feel, stronger than any
A knot tied us all.

My impression of them
Sweetness of beautiful turtles
Creating sounds of music
All to have joy from
Music to each
O! Such a sweetness!!

The first man their leader
Is a God Fairy cherishable soul
His tone never strong or light
His talent second to none
A manner of a Solomon
And a heart of Jesus
This man stands
Amongst the tallest of men
Yet, not of size
But of stature.

The second man is music
Quiet, but sure to make a point
A Don Juan he can never be, yet
A Prince to the letter
In time of need, always there
Ready and willing
Oh! my second turtle of music men.

This gentleman, the youngest of them all
Flexy and carefree
Unassuming, but never bottomless
A talent is seen
The star sparkling upon his brow
In there a star is being born
Oh! my third turtle of music men.

Here the fourth and quietest of the lot
Daring
Never cold
Tiger to his work
Oh! such a man, for without him
Sweetness of the bunch is gone
Oh! my fourth turtle of music men.

Here are my turtles of music men
Never moving more than they have to
But with music and mixing of sound
Forceful
Quick
Like a deer in full charge
These men are bold and astute
Cherished and adored
This world would be
Stronger for love
Respect
Talent
If my turtles of music
Could sprinkle their
Seeds upon us all.

To my friend and client Peter Max.

A MAN OF LOVE

Through the years in life
many
have been called Peter.
In The Bible, the book of wonders,
is our most famous.

Yet, through decades
there has arisen
a name,
a creation of a style,
a technique
in the world of art and dreams,
Max, who did touch us.

HIs chosen work
rewarded him, but best of all
    touched us.
All the world always has
    ugly knaves.
His idea is having
flowering love and devotion.

He walks with all, never losing
    his touch with life.
He makes you glow with inspiration.
He makes you bleed with love
    for him and all
your body quiets itself and
    huddles in contentment.

Colors of the rainbow
Spheres in the night
Bridges in the sky
Abstract delegates of the universe
he creates.
The mightiest of men,
Yet his brush
is oh, so gentle.

His manner is of a still, July night.
   still, July night.
His humor and delight of
   Spanish Fiesta.
The sorrow he dreads
All men count with him
but name too much of too little

This creator of pleasure for all eyes to see
With his love
shall
melt all the guns
and destroy all the hate
and war will be just a word
with no meaning
As all turn to love
the flowers will bloom
the children will play
all will sing
the joys of life's love.

He shall make us all love,
not for just a day,
or a speck of a decade
Which will turn into a lifetime,
and death will be sweet
because of this.

He has given us himself,
for all to create in their minds
In their thoughts
In the warmth of summer
In the twilight of life.

This man Peter
will live in the firmament
   of immortality
Caressing the shoulder of God
on one side and caressing
Venus, the sign of love,
   on the other.

He is Peter
A vital creature of love
whose life is just beginning
Who gave us himself
for love
for respect
and peace.

ROSI VELA BY BERT STERN

To a client and friend—Joey Mills, make-up artist.

HEY JOEY

Make her beautiful, change her eyes
The words echo through his mind
He is Joey
They all say to him, you did and he did, Joey
He creates beauty, desire from the ordinary
He creates the love of beauty
Joey does.
Sincerely caring about changing a face
He adds the touch of glamour with his hands
and creative mind
He transforms the dull into warm beauty
Delighting in the sight of
the radiance he has created
They all love his touch
His delicate hands
And sense of beauty
There is only one Joey
The man who creates beauty
From the commonplace
This extra-seeing type of guy
J O E Y ! ! ! ! ! ! !

THE REST OF YOUR LIFE

We all take everything for granted
Our health
Our love
Our God
Our Being
    and ourselves.

Why is this?
Why is this done?
Does it have to exist this way?

The way we say 'rest of my life'
are words we take for granted
Their meaning granite to us all
and, yet, we take this as a bottomless truth.

Oh, the meaningful life we live
gives us what we give to it

The words are strong
    and full
Even if for a day
    or an hour
    For the rest of our life
    is tomorrow's beginning
    and today's yesterday

WORDS HAVE TOO MANY SHADOWS

His voice was soft yet strong
His tone was easy to listen to.
His face had lines of life and love
And his spoken word was often heard

People believed in him
Needed him
And wanted him
For he was their leader

His words through years
faded into darkness
All felt, in time
that his words had too many shadows.

To my clients and friends—
Dr. Buzzard and the Original Savannah Band.

THE BAND

Many of us hope and pray
That the day will come when
Success will
Touch our door
Caress our eyes
And dry our tears
To the awakening of a new life.
This life to them, the six I met,
Was their world of music.

They never had much
They came from the side of the
Track that
Nobody tried to remember
Their look was of clean America
Their education was astute
Compared to their background
The gutter was their friend,
Not of filth but,
Of play and song.

Each was a family
A huddled mass
Divided into one
Yet their achievement of gold
Was creating a place of music
In our hearts and minds.

Their leader was a tall, lean stick
With God's gift of music
Creating and producing sounds of the universe.
His heart loving yet always on guard,
Waiting to trust and love his peers,
His voice low and soft
His eyes warm and gentle
Oh, such a man, this leader of the band.

This second man of words
Always creating the language of art,
Seeking for learning and adventure,
Making the spoken word a beauty of joy,
His tall slender body always
Swiftly reaching to help another

His goal, his achievement, is greater than the band
He is the master of words
He is the sheriff of the music band.

This little lady of the band
Her voice strong and gentle
Captivates each muscle of your body
With her tones and her charm.
She is pleasant to adore,
Charming to be with,
Exciting to watch,
Like a beautiful nightingale
Like a Grecian urn
This sweetness of the Daye

This member of the band
Is quiet, with his heart of a lion.
When he performs
All eyes turn toward him
His astute words and experiences
Are endearing to the band
His presence is wanted and needed

His sounds are heard
His tones are never lost
His presence always felt
This master of the drums
A pleasure to his family
A credit to his trade.

This last member has guided the band
From the first day of the story book,
She has taken them under her wing
And cherished them
Her tears are not in vain
Her charm has held the band together
For truly she is part of the band
If only to encourage and
Stay with them through all trials
This sweet lady of the band.

What I have written—
A story of a band?
No, but of people
Who create a band
Make it breathe
Make it laugh
Make it cry.

They give to us all
Sweetness to hear and
Remember, words of charm
The soul of life,
The soul of the heart

They have given us themselves
And ask little in return,
Only you, the people, the mass.
They are the band of the people
For each of us, for all of us.

A DARING MAN

When first we met
I wondered
Can this man of men
Exchange his life
And his ideals
With people?
He need not
His life is too vast
Too complete, from within

I've met him, never
Wanting to get too close
As to his personal feelings of
    companionship
Only time can bring us together
His bearing strong and firm
His desires gentle and endearing
His thoughts simple but knowing,
Knowing where he came from
And where he is going.

His greatest glory is from the sea,
Finding in its depths
The secrets of true living
In as small a thing as a shell.

His friends are dear to him
    and adore him
His bold strength
Guides them and helps find their life
This stature of a man I met.

Yet, he has comforted me,
For no one will harm him
    or harass him.
His trouble is mine
His love is his, yet I know
    I am part of it.
His thoughts come from his soul
Deep from the root of his Dad
Whom he so loved and cherished
His companionship and tenderness are within me.

I shall not forget him, or he me.
We both shall walk in the rain
And not get wet
We both from within are in
Need of each other
Whatever each may be, space and time
Will never part us
Our friendship will bind us as one.

To the late actor James Dean.

ONE MEMORY

Darkness spread over the mind of the world
Suddeness of death was on the stage
It brought ominous fears to many.
Here a man to some
A boy to his sought to-be family.
Departed from our world of being to immortality.
Its mystery like that of himself,
His thought of death made his mind wonder how exciting it was.
To know it; to be a part of it.
He has conquered his endeavor that all men dread,
Death is now his friend.
What sort of person can he be?
His years were not ripened.
The world and all its luxurious goods were at his tips
Excitement he did crave,
But not to the end degree.
His moods made him excell from others
A quaint smile to be polite, yet boyish.
Does one want to know such a person?
To be a part of him.
Yet his voice can not be heard.
A laugh can not be sounded.
A tear can not moisten his cloth.
Just his memory to linger in the mind.
Soon this will vanish,
And only darkness can be seen.
Tis true we all have felt him.
Been a part of him,
He was all of us,
Put into one,
To be remembered as long as one has a thought of him.

To the late Judy Garland—Thank you.

HER LAST CURTAIN

Years have passed
Your song
Your smile
Your little voice
   Oh, such a sound
Heard by all
   for joy
   for tears
Only through you
   Our Judy—Oh, such a Judy.

The world would close its eyes
   to you
And listen
For the sweetness of you.
You gave to many
   your all
But we only took from you,
   Never giving in return.
   For our Judy—Oh, such a Judy.

But now, the curtain has
   come down
We know what we have lost
But why, always like this
To the bottomless, to the dead.
Then we cherish
Then we miss
Then we cry
Then despair!
For you Judy—were life
   were song
   were laughter

Anything else, we shall forget
   and have you.
Your twilight was not seen.
There shall never be a
   last curtain for
   "Our Judy"

Thank you, for your life
you gave us.
    But best of all, for
being you.

To the late John Lennon

HIS SONG IS HEARD FOREVER

The world was in need
The people wanting,
never knowing what it was
It came about
Swiftly and real

The sound was clear
It made us forget
the everyday troubles
The need to forget
the need to dream
the need to transcend

It was their music
their creation
and what a creation
This group of four
astounded the world
actualized their values

Now there are only three
God has asked for one
An untrue death
never desired
but made real.

A man of peace
a believer in truth
and pure feelings
Away from society
living for all
wanting for all
his ideals

He is gone now
but only from the earth of mortality
He is with us
till the end of society
For his music lives within us
eats with us
sleeps with us
He is the fruit of our life
and the staff of our youth
his song and songs
will be heard forever
and ever.

To the late actor John Wayne.

THE BIG FELLOW

Passing by life's way
It seems it was yesterday
For yesterday's ways are today's deeds
This big fellow made me laugh
At his casual tidbits
Made me cry when things were at a back end
This he did, gave a little of himself
This big frame with that sly smile
Will always be remembered
His strength, his presence, will endear him
He could make a sixty second appearance
   Have a remembrance of a distant mile.
He walked with the crowds and never lost his feelings
   or touch
This big fellow is not lost
He is just beginning tomorrow in the bright sky.
But, big fellows are a dying breed.

To the late Senator Robert Kennedy

MY FALLEN SENATOR

Oh such rejoice
The struggling
The sweat
The tears
We have won
A chance to be the
First Man of our country

The crowds were there
costumes of many
Laughing, Joking, Tears of Victory
Yet the assassin's aim was point blank
He was hurt, Maybe killed, our Senator.

the joy turned to sorrow
The laughter to tears
The tears of joy to that
of sobs of despair.

Why?
His life so young
Oh, what a life
So good
Now so bad

Our Senator
Our father
Our son
Our friend
Our next President?
Our enemy
Yet he is dead.

Why does this happen?
His smile to warm your heart
Sincerity to the depressed
Love for his wife
Love and affection contained only for his children
Sorrow he has had
But now, why?

Oh Father, Dear, God,
Please caress him
Cherish him, Ask him for our forgiveness
Shall he be remembered
Yes,
Yet our fallen senator
He has walked with Kings and
Never lost his touch with
common man.

Please forgive us
He left us much
He need not
He had all
Yet he gave to us.
Oh, our Fallen Senator

To his wife
his children
his family
his friends
his enemies
none wanted his death,
Yet evil did.
Please may he rest in peace
and remember us, as we
Remember him
Our Fallen Senator.

FAREWELL TO A DREAM

Today the storm came,
Its gust strong and to the heart,
Without a warning
Like a fickle lady
    wanting, desiring

This dream of no meaning to many
Yet life, to my heart,
Something I feel,
Something I know,
Something of Love.

Small talk creates many a struggle,
Many a tear.
Why should this be?
For you and I create and destroy
A thing of beauty.

The dream of yellow and green—
Such sounds of sweetness
Dissolved
With the stroke of the spoken word.

How does one say Farewell?
How does one say Goodbye?
To a life!
To a love!
To Success!

Or does one say,
Farewell good friend
Or just—Farewell
    dream of life!!

NEVER THEIR OWN MEN

All of us struggle for survival in life.
Some are fortunate
to achieve
A pinnacle of glamour
or success of one kind
or another
Yet, most…
I wonder!

I never question
That the sun will appear
or the sky is blue white
or the mountains are hard
and cold.
Yet, I wonder at these people.

Are they men
Or are they—"Never their Own"
Oh such words, said
With strong feelings
Yet true to the core.

Never could they achieve
Without others
Never could they do.
Without others
And never are they
Their own men.

Such a sorry task
But that is life
From first day till tomorrow
Never to change.
Power, money survive all
And, men like these never to be
   "Their Own Men"

To Broadway and its Broadway shows.

I SAW A SHOW!

I sat in my seat
Waiting
Expecting
The Uknown.
Only what I heard, hearsay.
The start, a beginning.

My eyes did see
My ears did hear
My thoughts did wander
For here were few,
Guys and Dolls
entertaining me
and having a ball.

Joy captured the stage
The sound of laughter swelled
As love was with us all
Sadness could never enter,
Their fun-filled tribe.

The show was different
I did enjoy it
Only because of them
they did fulfill each minute
    with sweetness of love
And a new understanding
This was the show to see.

I thank thee
One and all
For such a night, of sweet rhapsody
the show I saw brought to me
One night of fun.

Welcome to

The Yankee Stadium

"THE HOUSE THAT RUTH BUILT"

HOT DOGS 5¢

BEER 5¢ A GLASS
KNISHES 2¢

IMPERIAL THEATRE "PIPPIN"

featuring IRS

Bert Pudell
HONEST ACCOUNTANT

WE BALANCE YOUR BOOKS

INCOME TAX DONE
FRIENDS IN THE IRS
2 SETS OF BOOKS
WE TAKE FOOD STAMPS

PUBLIC BATH

HOT & COLD SHOWERS 5¢

ITS USE—MONEY

I walk down a street
its quietness does enter in my thoughts
a few hours—all noise
Movement
Talk
To ask, and not know.

Now its stores on this street
    are quiet
The material items shine madly
    ready to conquer your mind
The sweetness of the colors
Invades your eyes
Captures your thoughts
Contains you
All these the media of its use
    "Money"

Does its use bring honor
to some?
yes—
Even though not deserving
its use brings life
Containment
Respect
But not at all, honor, to one's self
For its use touches,
regardless of right or wrong.
To be without it many are called dead
To be with it many are called dirty
To be in the middle of the road, one never
    keeps it.

To much, the parasite ever grasping.

To know how to be content
Is the wonder of life
Is the rhapsody
For all to achieve
And not let its use—money
Contain the mind
the body, and you.

*To a former client & Friend—Carol Bayer Sager
and Marvin Hamlisch, a friend.*

LOVE OR MISBEHAVIN'

God gives to many
Sight of the sky; smell of fresh cut grass
Yet, we take time for granted
Never thankful for these wonders and joys.

It is similar to love and misbehavin'
Two people I know and care for
    with joy and love
take for granted
their accomplishment,
their gift of what was
    given to them

They bring to people
The happiness of forgetting
    the sorrow of their time
The luxury of wit and words
    which so few have.

The first of these two bandits
Is petite and fluffy
    as a puff of French cake
As sweet as the first bite
As talented as God's gift to life.
Her strength of granite reflected
    in the thoughts she pens
She yearns to be loved
Not by a ruler, but only a lover
Without a contract
Giving in return at times
Then, stopping, afraid to be hurt.
She is love
Her tiny body yearning to embrace
But misbehavin' in her search for money and fame
    for which she has first in herself.

Her mate, a gift, that God spotted
    and granted such a jewel
Yet he is afraid to be needed or loved
His only desire is the trouble of many—
    Money
He has so much that his talent supplies
Yet, he is poor
He is warm and gentle and desires love
But is afraid to be hurt or rejected.
As I look through my window
And see two people whom I love
They are what love could be

But they are misbehavin'
    to themselves and others.

Oh please let love
Give way to how you feel
    and what you both need
Never a soft word of goodbye
The tears sprinkle my cheeks
Having them love
As I need them as friends,
    they need each other
As companion
    lover
    partner
They have given to all
Much of say and words
Now the world wishes them
    love
    peace
    and each other
No misbehavin', just sweet love

From Carole Bayer Sager

Is it possible that a man, responsible for the business affairs of so many, Can be so sensitive ... so human ... so caring and so poetic.
I would not have believed it was ___ and then I met Bert Padell. How lucky you have an opportunity to meet him too!

Carole Bayer Sager

LUTHER VANDROSS
FOREVER, FOR ALWAYS, FOR LOVE

FE 38235
STEREO

SIDE 1
AL 38235
℗ 1982 CBS Inc.

1. BAD BOY/HAVING A PARTY 5:16 -S. Cooke-/
-L. Vandross- M. Miller- (BMI)(ASCAP).
2. YOU'RE THE SWEETEST ONE 4:47 -L. Vandross -
M. Miller- (ASCAP)
3. SINCE I LOST MY BABY 5:28
-W. Robinson, Jr.- W. Moore-
(ASCAP)
4. FOREVER, FOR ALWAYS, FOR
LOVE 6:24 -L. Vandross-
(ASCAP)

To a client and friend, Luther Vandross.

YOU

Many happenings occur in life
many people one sees
many tastes one acquires
with events of fear and sadness
But, almost twenty years ago
an experience
touched my life
my soul
my heart
You!

Your childlike humor
Your smile which lights up a handsome face
Your fame of granite
Your wit of daring delight
A seed from God's will
You!

A man with family loves
A mother always by his side
Ready available, to teach, help
Through life's joys and pitfalls
A sister always caring,
coaching and yearning to assist
Their tears of delight for him
at success of his wants from life
This is you!

God gives and takes
some are gifted and special
While others just exist
Here the light appeared
It shows on your face
You!

To Luther Vandross.

IT SAID:

You shall give to the world
love, song and wit
You shall make everyone
Smile and cry
Through you, they will
forget the gloom of life's woes
You shall create
And, I will give unto you
the gift of inspiration
For you should come unto me
And make all hear the thoughts
of music, deep from within
You will walk in the rain, yet never be wet
Your soul and voice shall be my messenger
For all to hear.

To my friend Best,

I've come to unconditionally appreciate those things which have long term value. I've known you all my adult life and much of my younger years, as well. I'm proud of that. You've been more than a freind to me. You've taught me a lot and for that I sincerely say "thank you."

Best wishes for continued happiness. And, I'm proud to be a part of your new book —

Be Well,

Luther Vandross

123

To a former client and group I knew.

I HEARD A SOUND

I sat in my seat
waiting
Not knowing what to
Expect.
They were there,
Ready to proceed,
To entertain, or what?

The theatre darkened.
Silence filled the mass area
Then, screams and shouts,
    "We Want You"
Repeated, chanted over and over.

My mind descended.
Why did I
Bring myself here
For this type of atmosphere—
Oh, for What?
Then they began
With a loud sound

It grew louder and louder
And returned to capture
My body.

The performers on the stage
Created and brightened my thoughts
With their music to their vast audience.
The beat grew with each song, until—
I was with it,
With mind,
With heart,
With being,
Moving with the music
With the sound.

This created them on the stage
And I responded with the message
    "Rock On"
For the music had me
And the sound became part of me.

The sound was with me
My ears tingled and felt funny—
For the first time
My body moved, unchallenged,
My hands began to chant with the rhythm
    of the music
My feet began to feel with the beat.

They have brought
Soul
Love
Understanding
With these wounds of music
O, such as I
Bow my head
To them,
For they have
A sound
That has made me still with joy and love.

I KNOW

I know
That you and I are one
Each of us never apart

I know that,
That my love
Will move water
And water will move ships

This is how strong
We are Together

I know that you know
Life Is Us
Together and never apart

The glow on your face
Is the smile in my heart, For
I know I love you.

HUMBLE PIE

To my rock music group—Humble Pie.

MY GROUP—THE PIE

During one's life
We meet
All kinds
People, sights
Love and hate
Yet I found
True people called "The Pie."

To each ear
One hears music
Hard and loud
Strong but sweet
This is "The Pie."

A Group of Four
Four in a bunch
Each as strong as one
Vital to the other
This is "The Pie."

Tall, not like a tree
A wavy forest below his nose
His voice hard and wild
Stentorian in front of his flock
A writer of the music
As well as the words
To create a feeling
Each ditty a story book tale
This man shall walk and be seen
He be, One of, "The Pie."

His voice one could never mistake
A joy to the world
His sticks heard from one end
    of your body to the other
His beat loved, tense—yet gentle to
    your ears
The willingness—to be together
His sound marches into stevie's rhyme
This man shall walk, and be seen
To be, Two of, "The Pie."

This man can not be mistaken
For his is a string vibrating
    fierce and loud
His voice heard throughout
Sweetness—oh—so—sweet
The sound of the group
He always guards from within
Strives for success, then himself
    but first the group
This man shall walk, and be seen
He be, Three of, "The Pie."

Not the youngest
The neophyte of the group
His voice low and tight
Yet strong, to the point
His guitar talks such notes
Until it cries
This man shall walk, and be seen
He be, Four of, "The Pie."

We have seen
A Group of Four
Each a talent to itself
Each move
Each a tear
To mankind
Their echoes shall be forever heard
TODAY
And YESTERDAY

For Yesterday's TODAY
Is My Group "The Piece."

As Humble As They Be!

To Earl Monroe, my friend

THE BOUNCE OF LIFE

The roar of the crowd
Was outstanding
One could not hear one speak
Yet, the sound was pleasant.
It was for him
And only him.

He had created this
The bounce of life
Giving us all
His antics
His way of playing

A twist of his body
A body of long lean muscle
Each part coordinated to his mind
Responding to the sign
At the right place and opportunity
His face gentle as that of a baby's touch

A voice never hard always to the point
Directly to you, never through a whisper
His only setbacks are through his legs.
Always
Knocked
Scratched
Knocked down
Yet ready, like a worn torn tool
For his next job.
Never complaining
Even in despair or hurt
Ready willing and able
To fulfill his responsibility
To his bounce of life.

This man is a rare pearl
To himself and especially
To his fans and the world.
A soft tone, but always
Carrying a big stick
A man to like and love
For us, to make our lives
A bounce of pleasure, because
    of him.

From Earl Monroe,
Basketball super star

Bert,

    In today's world of material things
and astonishing accomplishments, we sometimes
forget the smaller things which keep us going.
Throughout my professional career, it has been
rare finding someone like you, who seriously
cares for me both as a client and as a friend.

    "In times of trouble, and in times of Joy,
I'm glad there is You." A bit corny, but very
true.

Yours,

as always

Earl Monroe

From Alan Gordon—
famous song writer
(My Heart Belongs to Me, Happy Together, etc.)

Dear Bert,

    I just wanted to take the time to let you know
how much you mean to me. In life you are lucky to find
precious few friends. Bert, you have helped me establish
myself as a successful composer. You have stuck with me
through thin and thick. We have gone over the counter,
and under the wire. We are now very involved in our
first musical motion picture, "The Man Who Never Left
For Work". I know we will do many things together and
I always will be in your debt. Thank you for your wisdom,
compassion and understanding, and don't let 'em steal second!

Love and best wishes,

From Joseph H. Harris—
Commercial Artists' Rep. and friend.

Dear Bert,

    As you know, I sure as hell can't express myself
in words as well as you, but I'd like to say without
being too "Korny"--"Thanks for being Bert Padell", a
truly dear friend that I have and will always cherish
for as long as my weary body is allowed to be on this
earth. The only word that says it all is LOVE...and
believe me it's not too often that one man can say
that to another (without being called a you-know-what).

    The years go by, we get older (not necessarily
wiser) and we must never, never lose that love. With
that in mind, all the craziness we see and create in
this world can still mean something.

    Please send my best to Bobbie and the children
and wish them the very best for the coming year both
in health and happiness.

                        Peace,

*From Elizabeth Granville—
lawyer*

Dear Bert:

Alan Siegel shared _Who Am I?_ with me. I have reread the poem several times and find more in it with each reading. It is a highly sensitive and deeply personal piece. I was very moved and felt as if I had a peek deep inside you... and I like what I saw.

With all my love
and admiration
Elizabeth
Granville

From Lorraine Festa—
A client's daughter—her response
to my poetry

Dear Mr. Padell,

I just wanted to write you and thank
you again for the tickets to the concert.
I really do appreciate it.

Another reason for my writing is to
tell you how much I love your "words".
I often read poetry and enjoy writing
myself, yet I have never before met an
artist such as yourself. Your words have
such feeling and deep thought. Some had
sent a chill right through me; they are
really beautiful.

Thank you once again.

Sincerely,
Lorraine Festa
(Frank's daughter)

To Teddy Pendergrass, singer and entertainer and friend.

TEDDY

When first I heard
We will overcome
They were words to a people
For a period in life
An opening of a door
Not a crack but a beginning
This is Teddy

I never knew this person
Only by name
or association
Yet thrilled many
peoples of the world

His smile, smooth
His features clear and delightful
This is Teddy

His dialogue to the point
He never wants one to skate
        backwards on him
Always to the point
Right on to the truth
This is Teddy

Now for a while
there is a low
But he will overcome
for the love of his
Mother, his friends and fans
He is life
and will always be just that
Teddy.

To Frank Sinatra, thoughts from his friend and mine, the late Montgomery Clift.

A MAN NAMED FRANK

Through the years
His voice has been part of our life
his smile ours
his laughter
his tears
his loves
shared with us
Yet, ours never with him
This is a man named Frank.

His tender years
Many of the young
Did crazy eye him
then
Stop!!
A halt
For a man named Frank.

Then a friend named Monty
did appear
A new career
A new beginning
A new life
For a man named Frank.

Through the years
he gave joy and sorrow
To his friends
His family
    his ominous friends
But most of all
To a people
This is a man named Frank.

A world with millions
And such a wonderful lot
Can only love
Cherish
At times, hate
A man named Frank.

TO ASK FOR LOVE

To be wanted
each day of your life
Is the supreme lust of being

The wanting of love
is the passion of each of us
with small talk ever listening from within.

The sound and desire of her laughter—
Even if the words have no humor—
would comfort me and capture me

For love is asking and knowing each of us
Cradling our thoughts
Within a treasure chest of dreams.

Dreaming of sugar covered love for each other
Missing the sight of your smile
the tears of sorrow
the joys of love making
and the wonders of each other

Each into one
One into each
capturing our decision for each other,
This is love, such love of you.

AT LEAST YOU TRIED

You pack your life in a bag,
Ready for your chance.
A dream it has been,
But now a sparkle of reality.
The years of learning to be tested at a moment
All your hurts and travails come alive.
Life is on the stage; your life,
And you are put in the spotlight.
Your chance has come,
The adulation of the world before you.
Like the springs of summer, freshness captures you.
It has come to an end, decision is near.
The world itself has stopped for you,
As you wait for your life's desire to bloom,
Defeat can be had,
But there is always a next chance.
The biggest sign in life, you have conquered,
The chance of trying and being defeated,
As you stand and face reality,
You have faced, life itself.

To my dad I never knew.

MY LOVE FOR MY FATHER

I've never been too close
I've never seen your smile
I've never heard your scream, for my first hit.

But I know
And feel,
You do love me
You missed my youth
You missed me
But for us,
   I love thee as strong as life
   I love thee as the slowness of a tear
   I love thee for you
   And what I've missed
   Your closeness, you

But you, my father, are life to me.

141

To former President Nixon—
and what the Bibles says.

WHY CAST THE FIRST STONE?

In life one passes many phases
In order to know
What life is.
Such a strange word
With meaning, beyond reproach.
People are what they are
They talk
Smile
Laugh
Cry
Suffer
Mostly through their own choosing.
Choosing to suffer or cry?
Oh, but why?
To be so cruel
Especially to oneself.
But we all do
Never change
And never learn from such a happening.
Why if we are so astute
And wise in life
Do we not try to repent?
Love is so beautiful
So caressing
So endearing
And wanting
Reason, for this
Is only for one's ego and/or
Power,
From the beginning
It has been, and will be
Yet, such as we
Reflect our own.
Are we not wise
To say
Halt!
Stop
No more of this foolishness!
Why Cast the first stone?
Let us live, not in deceit
Or jealousy and envy.

And, yet let all men,
Alike to the bone,
Know that one is no better than the other.
And only through achievement and work conquering life's goal.
Not who one knows or what their color is, or religion,
Then no one will ever be able to
Cast a stone at another.

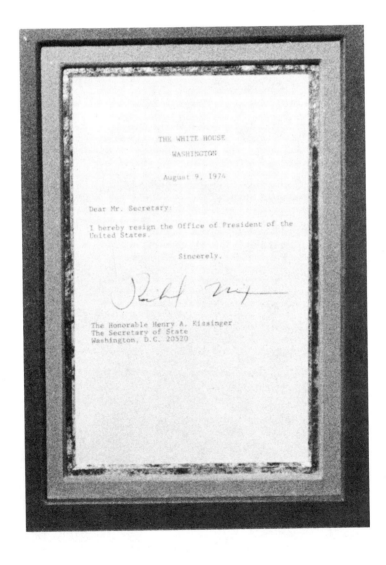

To former client and friend, Garland Jeffries.

GARLAND

He was a man from the streets
But, not as we think
Not dirty or crude or
cursing in his talk
He expressed his thoughts
through his songs
But this was a mask
to the world, and to himself
For truly he is
such a kind, lovable man.
The softness of his tone
is sweet as the nightingale
His wish to go forward
and strive to the top.
Is what all men desire to achieve.
He is true
For he is Garland
A man among tall trees
Sturdy during a storm
Always swaying with the wind
standing and absorbing
the fierce gales
This man Garland
Oh, such a man
A man's man
and a boy's dream
Garland.

GARLAND JEFFREYS
ONE-EYED JACK

145

To the late Gil Hodges of the Brooklyn Dodgers and manager of the NY Mets.

THE SILENCE OF THE DIAMOND

Each year when the "Robin" came
It was the sign of the time
The beginning
Of his life
The stage was to be set
Rehearsal was to begin.

Each year he did struggle
To achieve perfection
To hope he would succeed.
He fought hard
His hands strong and large,
Yet soft for those he loved.

He did entertain
For many came to see him,
Enjoy, yell and hope for him.
He achieved
What many wanted
It was his life, his wants.

When his time was up
To entertain,
He wanted to help
To teach, to have the strength of his career
Shine on others.

Now he manages many,
Tries to have them perform like him.
He is silent, yet strong
He has won, yet what!

For a sudden there was a warning—
Heed, he didn't
Stop, he didn't
But why!
This was Robin
And now all gone.

Such a man
A tulip in the sun
A daisy in the wind
All this
Still there.

And he will always be—
So long as they
Play ball—and the
Silence of the diamond never ceases.

Why there be white, black, yellow peoples
Why there be Christian, Jew, Protestant, Mohammed and Hindu
Why there be light, darkness
Why there be the bluest sky,
The greenest grass, love versus hate.
To ask is only to cause and ask But Why?

The good die young
the bad linger forever
The beautiful always know of it
The ugly never forget they are.
The rich cry of poverty
The poor can't afford to cry.
To ask only,—But Why?

The great wise men of the world
Never too wise to listen
Yet there are
Wars, killings, that never cease,
For people can't get along.
How can nations
But Why?

To cure
To stop
To relieve pain
Is God's gift
Yet this is always last
But Why?

To fight
To hate
To be angry
Are always partners
Yet love
Peace
Contentment
Never have a crowd
But Why?

A child,
A brother, sister, mother
Born from the same blood
Yet—jealousy, despair, always there between them.
But Why?

Money
The wanting of all
Desire of the world
The ominous touch
For all to desire, yet ugly knaves will always be there
Ready for the time to take,
But Why?

I stare out my window
The tears of the outside touch my window
      pane.
To ask please should this be
Let there be a wanting
      a love
      a desire
      a curing
      a helping
      to all
A life, this is precious
To be cherished as a rare jewel
To be needed
To be desired
To be tasted
To be warmed and loved

It shall come
my tears shall not be in vain
I can say, let there be good
      with the bad
Yet my friend shall slap my face
to make a point or take a dollar.
We can then ask "But Why?"
and the meanings will be few
for all will be answered,
and that will be life itself.

Thanks to the Bronx, Creston JHS 79 and Club and friends "The Flicks."

THE NEIGHBORHOOD

The yells and screams are gone
The games at night are quiet
The talks in bunches are not heard
"Johnny on the Pony" games are a whisper
My heart is still—for
My Old Neighborhood.

The streets were always noisy,
laughter was not a stranger
To walk on a hot summer night
was your only pleasure
To assemble on the corner and
meet a friend was life
Oh—my Old Neighborhood.

Dancing in a park was the thing of the day
To play in the school yard, many
   watching, was to have a perfect day.
This has been wiped clean
from my old neighborhood.

The streets are quiet
Noiseless of boys and gals
But why?
For this neighborhood
brought me to manhood
created me
cultured me
caressed me
Oh, but why all is changed
As if, never been
The spring of my youth
   is the streets, the gutters
the halls of the buildings.

It has given me love
To know
A prize of youth was my
   Neighborhood.

To NY Yankees baseball star—
the late Thurman Munson.

A TRIBUTE

During one's lifetime
The necessary acclaims occur
We are part of them
On purpose or as a command
The willingness of one's attributes
    We allow to fade with time
These aspects of life
These ventures and deeds
Are usually never saluted
    nor acclaimed during our lifetime.

It takes the leaves of seasons
For man to pay tribute for one's honors
Such as for health, love, honor itself and
    peace, sports, etc., etc.
Yet, why are we part of this falsehood?
To admire, respect one's ability
Should be for the living
As well as the dead.

Such waste
Such bottomless
Nonsense
To be guilty of this

To pay tribute to a person
As his deeds are being accomplished
Is the way of the living
Time is so short
In one's lifetime
We all have to fill it
With each second of a distant run.

Recently, we all lost a fine competitor
A man for all seasons
A leader to all his men
A father to his children
And a love to his wife
He was above the norm.

Yet we all took it for granted
As if reading a daily newspaper.
It will always be there, why not?

Shall we all change?
By paying tribute to the living
Acknowledge him for giving us part of himself
To the many
And leaving the few who love him
Share only days with him

What he has given us is priceless
Kings could not buy
For he has given us himself
A tribute to a man

To trees on the Major Degan Expressway.

A GARDEN OF TREES

They stand so tall in the breeze,
The big and small, swaying with each gust.
Their firm grip upon earth;
To stay, as long as time permits.
Some are cut before their time.
Dying, they gasp for air.
The bright green they once had—
Now is a sickly and colorless hue.
Oh, so bold a tree I see,
With its make-believe manly desires for life.
Its grasp bor heaven's caress appears
To ask for life.
This garden of trees my eyes will ever perceive
For rich or poor, this wealth of beauty is here
Time does play a game with them,
Their way of life will always be seen to man

To Armand Braiger and Mario De Martini,
owners of the restaurant—One If By Land, Two If By Sea

TWO BOYS

Time has brought into my life and family
Two boys, two men,
Two hearts, two souls
that God has given.

Never selfish
Always caring
Never crude
Always helping
Never loud
Always gentle
Never they first
Always you and yours first.

I can never match or repay them
Only thank God
I've met them
And need them, and want them
for what they are to my mind and being.

They are me
Two boys
The dearest
For they create love and feeling
   in us all.

DEAR BERT,
   THE BEAUTY OF YOUR WORDS FILL OUR
HEARTS WITH JOY AND LOVE. SHARING YOUR
WISDOM, SENSITIVITY, WARMTH AND UNDERSTANDING,
HAS ENRICHED OUR LIVES BEYOND MEASURE.
   THANK YOU FOR BEING SO GENEROUS WITH YOUR
LOVE AND LETTING US BECOME A PART OF YOUR FAMILY.
WE LOVE YOU VERY MUCH.
                              ALWAYS,

To L.P.

THANKS FOR THE CHANCE

We are told to turn the other cheek
to forgive our neighbor
Dear friend
You have given me
a spark of hope
Maybe just for days
or minutes
or seconds
You stranger
I will never forget
I am innocent
Free of wrong
Yet, you question
and give me a chance
to prove it.
It has taken almost half a decade.
My body
My mind
have deteriorated
It is all like a bad dream
Yet, if the answer is bad
I will never give up
my innocence
And free will of thought
For which you, kind soul, have given me a chance
I thank you for the dream
I thank you for the kindness
I thank you for this
Complete stranger
Thanks and thank you to God.

To Alan Grubman and Arther Indursky—
entertainment lawyers and their friendship.

TIME BETWEEN FRIENDS

Time is never an enemy for friends
It is swift for those who don't have each other
It is slow for those who are fortunate enough
To be friends
For time will always be our partner
We fear not, nor grieve from despair
We rejoice
We laugh
Because we know and have
Our sincere friendship for each other
There is always time for us
Because of our love and devotion
Friendship is our only measure of time
Through you and me
For you are my friend, today, tomorrow
      and next time around.

WHERE AM I NOW

Where Am I
I am here only because of you
My dear, my dear love

Where Am I Now
because of you
Love of mine
When you smile
my heart double beats
Only because of you dear

Where Am I Now
Where Am I Now

I am here now and forever.
My love for you
Is my love for my life.

THE TRUE MEANING

I ask myself
gazing out my window
as the day turns to darkness
and the darkness to light
What is life?
What are its standards?
Its goals?
But most of all, why is it?
And what makes us laugh and cry?
Life with its glorious scenes
We all try to be part of
success and love
And many fail.
One true meaning of life is to have
A person who will never say "no"
Even though the feelings command
And the atmosphere says "no"
You, my friend, are the brother
I always sought
My love will be with you
Until God separates us
The word friend began with you
Until God separates us
The word friend began with you and
My love, devotion, sincerity are
the true meaning of what I feel for you
My dearest friend.

SILENCE

Today I sat on a bus,
an everyday bus,
No different from any other.
Yet, this man sat next to me,
Different
From yesterday,
For he had silence in his ears.

The bus, oh what a bus,
moved on, stop by stop.
He got off this bus,
and another appeared and
    sat next to me.

He, too
was silent,
Unable
to hear the wonders of the
    busy city.
I realized today
    am I lucky or what?

They are all deaf.
Not just in hearing,
but deaf to my
inner feelings,
happiness
and deep love.
Yet, I would open my heart
    for them to capture my sorrow
and hope this world of today
    would be my life of tomorrow.

To Lou, a friend I thought I had but lost.

A FILE

When first we met
It was strange,
A loudness
Wise remarks
And no gentleness
ever appeared.
Yet, something was there.

His appearance
not striking
but pleasant
A handsome man
He knew he was
that was his problem
His confidence
Yet One could feel his lack of life
Always thinking someone was
Ready to knock him down

Beat him
Steal from him
Leave him
Laugh at him
Oh! such a pity
For this man of confidence

Friends, he knows not
What they are
They are not the ones that
gave him their hands with wet palms.
Ready at any given time to slip away.

The friends that love him
he destroys
Hurts
Just like that of his loved ones
We adore him
Cherish him
And deeply love him
Only to play second to
Unknown knaves

This is a file on a body
A person
who hurts many
And through the years will continue
In the same vein.
Yet, maybe
Someday
The firmament of life will
Awaken him
With a touch
And say
The ones that love him
Caress his eyes
Kiss his eyes
Because they are his light
Which will transcend into
His body, his heart and soul

Only to know, they love him deeply
And hope someday
Life will only
Be filled with love
From him to them
Forever and ever
Till death does part us all
for a movement
Only to awaken in dreams
Wanting love

BEING ANGRY

The center of Life is love and contentment
We try to abuse this
Caring only for tranquility of life.

We all love this prospect of serenity
But we are human
And we need to cry
Whether for happy times, distress
     or anger

What is anger?
When it first appears
We all use it and abuse it
Many times, we say things
     and do things
With the voice of anger
Projecting ill feelings,
dissent and prejudice
We mortals, oh what fools!
To be angry at times is
     good for the soul
But, only for the moment
Never to linger on
Let it vanish, for it is only a
     temporary disturbance.
To be angry now and then is life
And life is what we all live.

WHAT DO I WANT?

What do I want
from life on earth?
I want to have my mind free
from strain,
not of work
or long dreadful hours,
but small talk of my love.

When first we met,
life was full of love and want.
But now, I feel I am in a box,
never knowing when the lid
will close in on me.

Why should this happen?
to anyone.
Love for life
Love to be loved by one
is, oh, so wanted.
So needed.

But, her talk and feelings
  have changed.
The attitude of life
is that of a robot machine.
This can never be.
Love must be free
especially for me.
If not, I am not a man
to myself.

I want love caressing each
  minute of the day,
with or without her, knowing
that it's there ever waiting
  for me.

I want my life to exist
    for her,
but also to exist for me.
I want her to have interests
    in life,
in dreams,
in expectations,
in desires for me.

Life is what one
    takes from it.
She is her own,
I am myself.
Never changing each other.
Only compromise for
    one another.

If there be no retreat
    by her,
this ever shall increase
Tis sad, I shall have
a regrettable task, never
    to turn back,
Wishing her good cheer,
good life,
much love.

I shall walk in the sun
This task is burning,
through the sun's rays usually
    blind me.
Not today.
My mind clear and wanting
Knowing that what I do today
Will enclose and caress
    my future.

THE MAN THAT IS ALONE

The room is occupied with people, yet I am alone,
Their laughter is a faint sound to me
I pretend to listen; my thoughts are distant.
To have this feeling disappear is all I want
I wonder, Am I always to be alone?

167

*To Susan, my former girl-friend
who loved the Dance.*

LIVE TO DANCE

I sat in my seat anxiously waiting curtain time
This high massive veil will soon be swept by for all to see.
Stillness was suddenly present
It had come—the time was here,
The dance of dancers was to be seen.
Applauds they both do entertain
Not deserving as yet,
But theatre; the curtain
Music
At last their challenge.
As I watch so humbly
My heart felt faint
My eyes closed,
I was on the stage
Suddenly the music leader; with a loud hoarse, but mellow sound
Reality and back to earth I did descend.
Tears to my eyes
How wonderfully they perform
Each movement a rhapsody
I looked at each of them more seriously than ever.
The greatest height of all dance,
Is the seconds of suspension between movements
Actual coordination, interpretation of the dance.
Each dancer tries to inject this into his audience.
The dancers' eyes seemed to feel the music
With each beat their magnificent body responded.
It seemed to be one—the dancers and the music
A feeling of splendor, accomplishment they had won
Each wave of music they interpreted to their feelings.
They have conquered their audience
Not as a savage or suitor in battle
But with sudden enchantment
As if a rainbow had suddenly appeared,
And shown a beacon on them.
This is but one performance
One rhapsody of glory.
Yet as they live only to dance
All pray that such a gift,
Will always be seen, loved and enjoyed in the hearts of all.

Inspired by THE THREE DEGREES
performance in Nottingham, England, 10/24/79.
To Richard (Manager), Sheila, Valerie, Helen-

PEOPLE I REPRESENT

The years of my life
   pass me by
Looking in the mirror
   of what I've done
I see what I've tried to do

This part of my life
   is dear to me
Only because of them
   and them only

Many are foolish
Many are sad
Many will be crazy
But, all in all,
   the bloody bunch is terrific

They all perform from
   their souls and hearts
Whether for one
   or a million listeners
Only to please and perform
Whatever these private feelings
The risk is always there
A dim chance at that
That they will ever make it.

All of them have inspiration
They perch on life's branches
Sensitivity may be their only ability
The knowledge that, win or lose,
They must try.

They will never change
Neither will I
Their scramble in their careers
Is a must, is their life.

These people I represent
People of love
Compassion
Desire
Hope
From me to them
The people I represent

TO BE AFRAID

To be afraid of what will happen
Is darkness and cold
Why deserve such an ordeal?
I am a good person
I believe in people
In love
And respect
And in God
Yet, I am afraid.
I shiver with goose flesh
But I will conquer
this, being strong
from within
My strength will come from my family
and from God
The coldness will thaw
and be replaced by
the warmth of a Palm Springs day
I will endure
and my body will be smooth
and warm again.

A trilogy—a story of life
between a father, a mother, a son—
in Nazi Germany.

LIVE WITH HATE!

Today I come home to mourn
My beloved mother who has gone to immortality.
Her love was at a distance
Why?
Because of him—my father.

The hate in by blood is thick,
Only for him.
He caused it—
Her death—my mother, my mother.

Turned on his friends,
Shamed his family blood.
All this to protect his own skin.
The hurt he has caused can never be undone

My money he abhors, yet he takes it.
He takes it to feed his belly.
If men were tried on thoughts, I am a murderer
My love he has destroyed.

(continued)

TO SPEAK THE TRUTH

The years have parted us, my son.
Your hurt is deep because of me.
This wrong I cannot disclose,
As I thought time would vanish this ugly past.

It seemed to be a dream, but reality overshadowed it.
That tempest night, my beloved wife suffered.
Her cries of horror still conquer me; helpless as I was
I must forget, or forever be a stone.

You come here today, with the heart of a mad dog,
Vengeance is the only reasoning your mind captures.
Your harassed attacks upon me,
Have made life more unbearable.

Tis not easy to repent,
But why do you accuse, without asking the truth?
My sin has been for her sake,
And there has been no sin!

My son if my heart could speak,
You would hear no wrong
There is none to tell, just coarse talk.
Life could be new for you and me.

IF I HAD KNOWN

What have I said?
The words he cannot forget,
They're imbedded,
If only—I had known.

Tis not late, I pray,
To touch him, and have his love tingle within,
To have us watch summer change to autumn,
Then together, as father and son, endure the winter.

YES OR NO

This man has a job to do
Different from most to conquer and endure.
He tries to listen and understand
the words of men
Many who appear before him
talk of ugly knaves
He walks with kings but never loses the
special touch of decision.

His choices are difficult
For he must prosecute
those he thinks
have done wrong
Yet at times he is mistaken
This he must live with
Oh, such a man
to endure this ordeal

He must make a yes decision to hurt someone
He must make a no decision not to hurt someone
This only Solomon from the Scriptures needs
Yet, he accepts this burden

He is young in years
But at times old in ordeals
His family loves him
He wants only right to prevail
Ever hoping not to err
Oh such a man, with such a burden.

We cannot deal without him
Let God guard him and lead him
Hearing all
and with God's help and himself as a fair man
Coming to the point of yes or no.

His statue will prevail
for he will walk through the rain and the storm
And not get wet or feel cold
for to him all men count
but none will tarnish his thoughts and ideals.

HOW CAN IT HAPPEN AGAIN

History
the word, the meaning,
is taught to all
memorized and often forgotten

Yet, we should learn from it
Its source
Its meaning
Its results

The erosion
The destruction
How did it occur?
How to stop it?
Why was it created?
Why and more *why's!*

We look in the mirror
The reflections are not far
Pure and not vague
Not like dropping pebbles in a still stream
Never seeing
a clear, clean picture.

Why does it have to happen again?
Are we not astute enough
Or, don't we care
Are we masochists
Or just too lazy
To see the hurt so many suffer?
Why??

Please stop them from pla ing the same song
With the same lyrics
Stop it
By the voices
of many—
Learn from the past
Don't let it happen again.

The test of a man
is the happening of the crisis
he endures
When ugly knaves knock on his door
When all men are counted
but none is very strong.

With the happening of the crisis
one reacts
and accepts
but fights on, not to despair
but with greater bridges
to build
And not to let sorrow and depression
be your partner.

That is the light and statute of a man
living and breathing this crisis
enduring and capturing and absorbing it
To make him the man he really is.

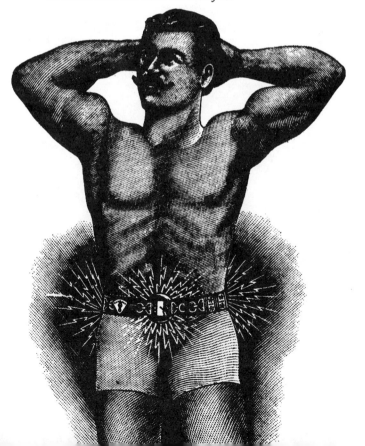

ONE DAY OLDER

I look back and see what I've done.
Is this year different from any other,
or have I, as a person, achieved
for myself,
my being, my life,
accomplishing what I wanted?

What is it I wanted?
For some, money, love, health, etc.,
for me, only and first for me,
belief in life,
in love, for what love gave me.

My health is the supreme of all
    my desires.
My belief in God and His being
    is enough for me.
For my life for all,
my life for my dear and close ones,
I am most grateful,
grateful to know and associate with them,
as they give me of themselves.

From these three sources of life,
I have power, money, etc.
Of all the knaves of life.
I am the richest, because all my
    desires have resulted in peace
    of mind and body to me.
Today I am one day older.

A MAN OF HIS TOILS

From the day of the first book
of words and deeds
Man was his own destiny
his own make of life.
He guided it,
constructed it,
planned it
designed it
built it, and destroyed it.

A man from the horizon
a simple fresh human being
of tales of his father
If only to transmit to his
children.
If only the children of
his life
could have respect, and if God
    should let
love be part of that respect.
This was a man of his toils
    I met.

His goals childish at times
but astute in his every decision.
At times hesitant to make
a right or wrong move.
Yet he has learned
It is better to decide mistakenly
Than not at all.
This main man of his
    beloved wife
A woman who has been a partner
to his work,
to his sex,
to his children
and especially to life itself and to him.
Life would stand still
if her voice,
her aroma,
her love were no longer for
This man of men.

I have met him
Respected him
Desired his talk
Desired his funny laugh
Respected his roughness of
    business
But relished his success in it.

He has made a mark
upon the page
The ledger of life,
Showing, what we all
have accomplished
His scale has the
print deep with ink
the substance ever flowing
This man of his toils
God will never forget
Nor will he ever be forgotten.

He will score and attain
all his desires
For, he is a man of the earth
and a main-stream for
all to reflect upon
This man of men.

To us all.

PRISONERS OF MONEY

As we travel through
   life
Many happenings occur.
We strive for deep and
    handsome success.
The struggle and deeds
    we try to conquer
Ever hoping to endure
    the hardship
    of life's ways.

Life is gentle
But we ourselves create
the bottomless pits
the crevices
the shadows
the loneliness
the silence
This is a part of the page
of life
The other is the success
of life itself
And do you or I become
this prisoner of what we all want—
    Money?

AT A FUNERAL

Ah, they were as comfortable as possible.
Their words
ever flowing with people, thoughts and deeds
when a loved one passes away.

The briefest thing we have in life is time
Such a commodity,
rare and precious,
Such a jewel to all of us.

For when God takes you away from
    The world of being
You reach a greater place,
The very firmament of life and being.

When you die, you are alone
Death is final,
everlasting
Time is the only shortness we have in life.

To a friend, my late dentist.

THE UNFAIRNESS OF DEATH

This night I wonder to myself:
A man not so close to me is dying;
The whole neighborhood is in a quandry,
For this man of once sturdy back and round full face,
    is now a weary tree in need of water.
On this night tears come into my eyes
For here is Man, a helper to Man itself—
For one to protect the young and old in time of need
A maker of teeth and a fixer to all.
The Holy Bible talks of "3 score and ten"
But this man is only 2 score and ten.
Oh but life is new to him
For a young man such as he, he has yet to live.
A father to his sons,
A husband to his wife,
A son to his maker,
And jewel to his mother.
Time is short, one can see.
Is one to judge how long he should live?
Is there a judge of all being to decide?
If so, please hear my plea.
For all of us born in turn reach the final resting place.
Rich or poor, colored or white, we all are the same—
God created us all thru the seven days of wonder
But the supreme make of all, is from whom being came;
    the sand conquers all.
I lift my head, and the tears are dry in my eyes.
To pray, to hope, is all I can do
To ask Him to be just
For You alone can save the man.

TOMORROW

Tomorrow will never be
Tomorrow will never exist
We must look only for today

We will live each second
each minute
each hour
for today
for life is for the living

and tomorrow will never be
if today we live and love
only for this day.

I COULD LOVE YOU

I could love you today and tomorrow

Till you and I are one
We both keep on together
The string is tied
The place is set
The time is now
For I can love you forever and ever
Till death does come
I can love you.

Love is the stars
Love is the sky
Love is my heart only wanting you
Asking only how I could love you
Oh, to love you each way
My thought of life
To love only you.

TRY TO REMEMBER

I look to the sky
And try to remember
That November will come
And will run into December
Where we all feel and want
Peace and happiness.

The feeling is there
In the air
In the heart
And mind.

Yet, the voice of my friend
Has made me silent.
Friendship to me
Is not a word
It is a feeling within,
A wanting
A caring
A needing.

It is not to smother
Or capture one
It is there,
A happening
A feeling to remember
Jealousy has no place
It should not overpower
One's mind.

Yet, try to remember
That to love
Is the most precious part of life

I ask you, my dear friend,
Whatever has happened or will
I shall not forget
The times of happiness
The times of joy
The times of folly
The few times of despair
Only because of you.

You have given me
And I have given you
Not for reward
But for each other.

Never let us lose this
In spite of ugly knaves
It is God's gift
It is our gift to each other
Try to remember when
November comes to December,
Try to remember....

TO DREAM — THE IMPOSSIBLE DREAM

At times in our life
We dream and wonder
Ever hoping
Expecting
Praying
Believing
For all to come before our eyes
Love everlasting
Time without end
Always hoping to dream
An impossible dream.
This dream of mine
I ask you, my God,
Whom I respect and love
And devote my life to
Please hear this one chant
This one desire
This one hope
Till the moment
When you shall call me
Grant this one desire:
May it be possible
My impossible dream.

SWEETNESS OF SUCCESS

The aroma of the air
The flight of its scent
Each nostril yearning
to enjoy,
Its wanting
desire
Its touch, if only for
a moment.
Ah, such sweet destiny
That it should capture
one's senses
and mind

My eyes will clear
as a beginning winter day
Its sureness
Its delightfulness
Strictly, there.

This sweetness
Is for me
My ego, my life,
my me, and only me first.

Then to you and yours
Such is my case
When the sweetness of success
Shall drop its toll
on only me
Oh, such sweetness
Success.

To scientist Albert Einstein.

THE CROWN OF SCIENCE

The sun has nestled for the day;
A world mourns this day of sorrow,
Many wonder to themselves, will there ever be another?
His kind and gentle manner far superior to many,
    his mind advance to unforeseen eras—
He has died, in the wakening of his discoveries.
His way of dress dear only to himself,
A world in his own, while a teacher to the world.
The dawn has come from his wisdom
As a new horizon has awakened
This man is not lost to the world; he will always
    have science for us to adhere to.

GOOD NIGHT MY FAIR LADY

The evening closes in with sudden darkness?
The day was brilliant, being with you.
But for now, time is short
For one to say, "Good Night."

TO CRY

One such as I asks,
Is there a place for crying?
Does it favor one or another?
Men or women?
Black or white?
Youth, or the old?

A man such as I
Cries
Only for the sake of a feeling.
One, such as I, has a deep
    endearing love and
Tears caress my cheeks
And capture my need
To escape, to cry.

198

THANK GOD IT IS NOT MINE

There was sorrow
in a small part of the world
Each of us cried
Yet your sorrow was untold
Unbearable, unfair
Yet, thank God it was not mine.

Your love for your little one
In the spring of her years
was cherished
Untold
Uncounted
For my little ones, they are my
Desire, my wanting, my life
Without them
It would be like a tree bearing no fruit
The sky with no light.
The earth with no air
Yet, Thank God it was not my loss.

Your loss will never leave you
You will live
Yet with death in your heart
Sorrow in your mind
Joy shall be a shadow
The living must live and the
    dead be a memory.
The twilight of her life had not arrived
Yet, Thank God it was your loss.

JUSTICE

Justice for all
A word used so often
But never considering
its full meaning

Justice is to be merciful
fair and discreet, also
cunning and astute.
Yet strong and delicate
precise and at times liberal
with a fair amount of conservatism

Justice isn't perfect
Is Justice to be done?
At all extremes
At all costs
No, what is more important
Is Justice of factual issues
You see the dead don't weep
We live for the living
and living Justice must prevail

Justice for all
For all skins and lives
But to remember the unforgiving desire
Justice for the living
Not for the past
But for today
and tomorrow's tomorrow.

To my son Scott—

WHAT MAKES HIM MY SON?

The quietness of his voice
Sensitivity to cry
Movement like that of a downstream
    brook
Freshness as, new cut grass
Shyness as a deer
Sureness as a Speaker of the House
Moody like that of a woman
Loving like God
Wanting like that of the mass
Yet one picture of him shines
At Thanksgiving,
The holiday of giving
Thanks to God
The cutting of the turkey
Oh, such a happy taste
He draws a picture of the bird
With many around to feast
Yet there are tears to the bird's eye.

This, my son, is real
This, my son, is life
This, my son, is you, and I
One, from the same cup,
    the same blood
Different minds, yet one
    heart.
What makes him—my son,
    Him.

I MISS MY SON

I sat in his room.
It was quiet.
The walls were silent,
Without the hammer of noise
Or the gentleness of his smile.
Oh, such a smile—
True, shy,
Without the cloud of deceit.
His bed untouched
still,
Waiting for him to return—

All his possessions
waiting
to caress him
hear his voice,
Yearning for his return
This house is not a home
without my son.
His presence
is ever wanting
is needed
is loved and most of all
is missed.
My Son—Scott.

To my son and all sons leaving for
summer camp, etc.

203

To Sarah, my late grandma.

I NEVER KNEW YOU

My life is what I have made it
I never blame anyone or any happening.
I am the creator of my deeds
My ideals and situations are my cause and effect.

In young and carefree years
I wondered how the sky was blue
the rain wet
the touch of her next to me
    making my body tingle.
To love—that was a word
to say, never to feel or want at the time.

That lady, so small in height,
so big in stature and in love,
Cared for all, but especially for me—
never selfish
always loving
And I, a child, never really gave anything in return.

The years have passed
And so has this lady of mine.

I think, if only I could have
    given what I know now,
not as child
but as a man.

I do love you, Sarah,
Grand lady of life.
Many of your virtues I now possess
Because of you

I never knew you until now
But it need not be too late
For my children and wife have your joy and love

Dear, thank you for what I know of you.
I will love you and treasure your memory always.

To my Dad—Love from me.

A STRANGER I NEVER KNEW

We each feel
   and desire
Love and companionship
When we are born
Desire for love
   should appear
But, human as we are,
   we let it dissipate
   and crumble
Foolish mortals we are
For this is the
   fullness of life
Yet we let a stranger appear
   between our circles of life

I knew such a man
A Father
A Grandfather
But why should this happen,
This nonsensical "Michigias"
Why, oh Why?

The desire for love
Is so precious
So needing
Yet time is a factor
The sixty second run
   is always years to come
Just strangers by day
   and a shadow at night
Oh, such a disappointment!

To talk with him
   for need of talk and wisdom
   like that of Solomon
And strength of David
   and desire and hunger
   of John and Robert
This could shine on him
If you be there this
   stranger of sort.

Comfort him when the cold is
    within him
Caress him when his first love
    is lost
Bless and lift him when his desires
    bring him to despair
Oh, this stranger of a man.

I hope I will miss these
    lonely days
My thoughts of him
I hope will never leave
Never to know if there were
    any good times, because
    of this space between us.

So this stranger I never knew—
My Dad
My love
My image
My heart
I do miss, the one I need and knew

WATER THE FLOWERS

In life we all try to water too many flowers.
Expecting to conquer
too much
Expecting too much love,
money and companionship.

We look in the mirror
and hope for reflections
of wholesome
nourishment of warmth and life,
Ideals of inspiration.
Yet—stop and
listen to life
Try to accept it for what it is.

We only get what
we put into it.
Not one drop more
Its thirst always there
Its desire ever hungry.

Just water the flowers
that we can reach
the comfort of the shore
of desire, that one can reasonably find.

Live for today, for each
day is a new beginning
A new life
A new flower
for us to water and appreciate.

Don't dispute your feelings
second chances are few
The garden of your choice,
in the flowers of today.
Enjoy and live to water the
flowers of life.

SWIFTNESS OF LOVE

When first my eyes met you
My heart acquired an extra beat
This never really entered my mind, that this would happen to me
For life as it was, just one big carefree ride
Not knowing where it would stop
Not Caring!
Suddenly it caught me
Without asking or telling
That you would be in my thoughts,
my aim and desires.
Your charm started to eat within my body
Laughter we both did have
Tears we both tried to conquer.
Just being with you made my day fulfilling
Our little talk
Carelessly found me falling in love
The swiftness of love made life more challenging,
To know that I have someone to share life with.

MEMORIES ARE FUNNY THINGS

The good times we had
I will never forget
The small talk
turning into love and passion
Your smile at the pleasure
I brought you.
The frown when naughty thoughts prevailed
The treasure of your face, that only
in memories I see
Memories are funny things
But they are the only life I have of you
My memories of you.

IN DREAMS

In dreams I create fantasies
of my love for you
In the mist of my eyes
I wonder about
making love to you
and having reflections
of you to me
and me to you
in my mirror of dreams.

TILL LOVE

Till love we first meet
I wondered at
A nothingness
To sink within
But then at last
I remembered
    my love, till life shall be
You shall be love to me

LOVE ME

Love me for just an hour,
Love me for just a day,
Love me for all my life
and I will be yours
     forever and ever.
If only just a minute,
My life will be a dream.

You are a part of me
     oh, yes, I do love you
With all my heart
caress you for evermore
And love one, as much as I love you.

My love for you is strong.
A tree in the wind,
A star in the heavens,
A bird in the sky
Can never be more
than you are to me.
Just love me,
If only for a tiny minute.

The day has come for us to
     say goodbye.
The nights will be a shadow
Without you, my love,
As I will always want you
If only in my dreams of love.

*To June Nadell, my friend and
my beloved partner and friend's late wife.*

SHE MUST LEAVE

Your love must leave you.
not for a while
not for a day
but for eternity.
Is this such an endless space of time
Or only a wink of an eye
A touch of a hair?

It is forever and ever
She will never return
Yet never will her love leave you

Oh, my life
Is gone
to despair
bottomless despair
rejection, blankness.

Yet, when I think
of love, it is she
When I think of life, it is she
Her smile
Her courage
the partner to my career
Our moments of love
Our hours together

She is gone from this earth
Yet she will always be with me
The rod and staff that guides me
Her love will envelop me forever.

She is myself
and she is all life
to me.

She has never left
I feel her,
I hear her
And I will forever and ever.

I love her and will always
She is my love
And death will not part us
My sweet dear love and I.

To my friends and clients, The Optical House—
Dick Swanck, Irwin Schmeizer, Sandy Duke,
Dick Rauh, Richard Rowholt and Willie Tomas.

THE GROUP OF SIX

To look back at time,
and wonder!
The pains
The tears
The worry
The wonders, was it worth it?
A story to be told.
Six men
of all sizes
some round, some tall
quiet yet loud and polite
Assuming, daring and boyish
Those were called "the group of Six"

Their main man of fame
tall and slender
his voice soft and not commanding
Yet such a sweet man
Simple but stentorian in character
A person for all to observe and notice in a crowd.

A maker of faces
A creator of lines and
Picturesque to all
Astute in mind
Mild in manner
A person for all to observe and notice in a crowd.

A wheeler and dealer
To obtain and acquire a place in life
A wanting desire to achieve success
A steadfast character for all to see
His smile as warm as his heart
A person for all to observe and notice in a crowd.

The smallest of the group
His ability never contained for a moment
His sureness never questioned.
His fairness always observed.
A person for all to observe and notice in a crowd.

The wittiest of the group
With his beads and colored cycle
Hours never frighten him to work
A soft and gentle man
A person for all to observe and notice in a crowd.

But, a man amongst men
Gentle and deserving
A spendthrift in nature
But willing to change
A person for all to observe and notice in a crowd.

These men started an empire

Harassed, bereft by suit and talk
By a Lord Barron so called with his
    only friend—"money"
Taken all in stride
To endure the cold hard fight
But only victory seen.

These men I don't love
But I caress them under my wing
To have success be their partner
    For the first time in life.
To have security touch their cheek.
To know to work hard, there is a reward
    and not just empty promises

This group of Six Men in a Crowd
Six in mob
Six for their place in life.
A life of love, health, contentment
    and honor with respect.

"My Group of Six."

THERE'S A LOT TO SEE

If you looked into the sun
your eyes would tear
from its rays
That is the same in life
If one looks fully into the span of reality
It hurts one's thoughts
Ideals
Pleasures
Disasters
Because it is real, it is life.

We all try to wear shades
Glasses to shield us
Yet. if we realize
Looking head on
At the situation
Knowing there is a lot to see
If one faces the sky and heaven
and knows He is always with you
Trying to help
Comfort and caress you
It is better to see each bush
than get lost in the forest
without a guide to where you are in life.
There is always a lot to see
If one will only look and be thankful for
what one has.

GIVE ME YOUR DREAMS

Each day of my life
I think of you
And hope you think of me.
This makes life so
captivating and real
Just you
Give me your dreams

A village in Club Med.

A VILLAGE

This place between life and love
Is a place in the sun
Each heart, open to each other
Each seed of giving, blooming like a
    flower in the sun
This a village I did visit.
There welcome beyond approach
A happening I never endured
Never felt or needed
They did conquer me
Within my eyes and heart
The art of giving
Even if just for awhile
The feeling there—
The air bright
With live, wanting
To be a part of
This village I did visit.

The eve of Christmas
They did invite many from a native village
The bright colours of their clothes
The colours brightest came from the children's eyes.
Their eyes of delight and sparkle.
They felt they belonged
Wanted,
The gifts of sweets, while love flourished
Within this village I did visit.
This village of varied tongues
With many faces
All, one thing in common
Peace, love for each other
being one group, within a village of love.

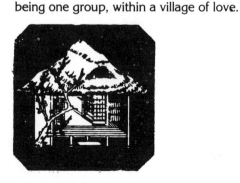

To my friend—
Gary Kurfirst.

YOU MY FRIEND

Time is the passing
of one's life
Some of us hear
The music of it
all the time
While others turn a
deaf ear
Yet if one is to find
one item in life
to treasure
it is
you my friend.

WHAT A CROWD

The roar came
The sound was overwhelming
Fulfilling
Its base came from within all

Its effect was an uplift
captivating your body
never a bottomless feeling
conquering your every thought
Oh, such a feeling

A feeling that each second captured
this is how it happened
That night
When they did "The Crowd"

221

"DONALD"

When she was, oh so young
Many did look the other way
Her lean tall frame
Her mountain-like cheekbones
Her oven deep eyes
Her sexual love
For this was "Donald"
A girl you ought to know.

Always ready for a smile
Always ready for love
Popular to many
But close only to one
Like that of "Aaron from the Bible."

To only know
This "Donald," oh, such a girl
For you to see
To admire
To Love
To dream of
and want
A sweet small smile
from her—for a gal called "Donald"

To my former secretary and all the secretaries of the world.

MY SECRETARY

To look around
and see time pass by
and now see what I've lost
not many realize
or appreciate
an important factor,
   my secretary.

My voice hard,
coarse at times
stubborn and never contained
   in my manner.
All my whims she caresses
for a job, a day, a buck,
for me
   my secretary.

When things are lost
she is the "Lost and Found"
When clients are in despair
she is their "Red Cross"
In need for help
she is my "Salvation Army",
   my secretary

Time passes
minutes turn to hours
days to years
never realizing
never knowing
of her help
of her sincerity
of her astuteness
of her friendship,
   my secretary

One is fortunate
as I
To have this woman
with me, at the start of
my career
   my secretary

The day has come
to say adieu
The sun is shining.
The days of life are hard
Movement of day is seen
Yet, she has been my
partner in thought.
She spoke for me
to many as if I had spoken
She has written letters with words of wisdom
    My secretary is leaving,
        from business to pleasure of married life.

I shall not forget her
Like a fine wine whose taste lingers on
Like colored flowers in bloom
with its colors captivating our mind,
LIke a spring brook running
downstream, its freshness
never leaving you....
Like a day should be, oh such a good day—
    to be alive.

Like two young lovers, their eyes
never leaving their sight.
Like God has given me your
    acquaintance, for two and a half years.

Are these feelings all from a boss
    to his secretary?
He can say "Thank You, a job well done."
But, I must say—"Goodby, Good Friend."

TO GOD

That lady arrived
Full of hurt and despair
Her cries of horror and pain
So underserved.

I, a stranger, wondered
Why?
Why such pain
For such a tiny body
Why such agony in
her slanted eyes?
Her cries of despair

Bottomless wondering
Why?
Fair or unjust?

God, I prayed, please caress her
Let her pain be soft and gentle

Reason is for the reasonable
But, there is no reason

She is so soft
Petite
Young
Pure
Let the light shine down upon her face
Make is glimmer with life again.

YOUTH IS WASTED ON THE YOUNG

Each day of our life
We reach for the pages of youth
Each hoping when reaching years in life
To have the calendar—time, stop

The foundation always running over
The stream of life, favor to some
Stranger to many.
Knocking and sticking at one's door
Knowing heartaches,
Distasteful fruits
Past and present
The time has come
They years have passed
Never to appear again
Not even for a flash.

One desire now
The want for strength of life
To endure immortality
The lines on one's face to disappear to dust.
As the mirror reflects only youth and
Desire for life.

The strain of life
The granite conquering of ugly gnomes
Your every whim
Youth and what it is—
To some, life itself
To others, a vase of living—a photo,
An instrument of being
For this desire
To have one dream—
Youth and only youth
It dissipates—for youth
Is wasted on the young.

ASK BUT WHY?

Through life
Each asks
But Why?

To have such an answer
To only know such a thought
To be astute
To be dumb
To be questionable
To ask But Why?
To watch lazy smiles
To watch their lazy smiles
Afraid to take it
As carelessness to the heart

or just the evasive way of a woman
Such charm when, they want, of desire
Is this woman?

To make love
Silence in nature, yet her smell whimpers
    your body
Her hand caresses your body
Her body firm and strong
Which only makes you stronger and desirous
Your lips touch hers and darkness captures you.
Your body intertwined with hers
Fulfilling all emotions
Oh, such a wanting.

For this is woman
At her greatest moment
A master to none
Loving and wanting,
She has made, asked
and known—That she is woman.

To Buddy and Lorrel Morgan—
a tribute to their late son.

A DOLLAR FOR JAMIE

I can remember
When last we spoke
His lovely smile,
His wanting to be with me.
Now he is gone,
Gone from the world of reality
Yet never from heart and soul.

Gone is a word
Oh, such a word!
Is a beloved gone when he dies?
Never!
They live within the person
Their face is her mask
Their ways and manners depict her
Which makes her live

Live for life
For it may vanish
Into just being a memory
Those memories do make up
    one's life.
One cannot live with memories alone.

Here, Jamie, when last we spoke
I owed one dollar.
I give it back.
Please caress my thoughts
Wherever you are.
This is our bond,
Never to be forgotten.
I do love you
For all my days
For all my minutes
For all my hours
All my life.

KEEP IT FROM BEING TRUE

I believe in God
I believe in love
in life and people
Peace and truth
for you and me
Whatever you do
or try to do

To change
to trouble
my thoughts
by evil deeds
and don'ts
I will never
accept for myself
as being the truth

For you are love
My love to you
The world and all.

THE TIN CAN

Common in nature
we all take its meaning for granted
for its need is only for the moment

Yet, there is much to see if you keep your head up.
For it quenches thirst
gives enjoyment of life
but always is thrown away
never to be touched again.

The rain wets its surface
The sun bakes its back
The wind moves it from side to side
The cold making it change color

We should see
this mainstay
of our life
always by itself
the lost tin can.

How a black man feels—
no different than a white man.

WHO AM I

My smile wants warmth
My hair has tint like the sky
My blood bleeds red
My hurt makes me cry
My tears make me feel bottomless
My love makes me tingle within
My hunger wants for taste
Yet I ask
    "Who Am I?"

The world we live in
Has the bluest sky
The clearest night
The coldest wind
The warmest sunlight
Spears in the night make ready
    for fire of mid-day
Yet I ask "Who Am I?"

My style is like yours,
My hunger
My taste
My wants
My desires
My love
Are like yours

When I was born
I was different
Why?
No thoughts
No language
No decisions
To be taught all these
Yet "Who Am I?"

My father, dear Lord, dear God
I ask.
My friend sleeps
He cares
He wants
He loves
Why is he different than I?

I love for love
My woman's aroma makes my body whimper
My thoughts of love are close and deep
My desire, my emotion, my wanting, my despair
Make me wonder, "Who Am I?"

The taste of sweet,
The careless feelings
The want of thirst
The smell of fresh cut grass
All these wants,I want too!

Am I different?
No!
My Lord,
My place is here
I shall make myself
Proud of it
I am "Who I Am!"

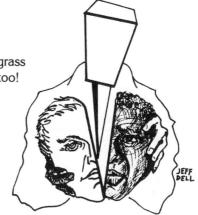

JEFF
DELL

I'D DO IT TWICE

We all want
Things and objects in life
Some of us need,
and some must have.
Throughout our lives
We'll go to all extents
to obtain them.

Yet
We look back
And see what we have
And usually say
If I had to do it all over again
I would,
But…"I'd do it twice!"

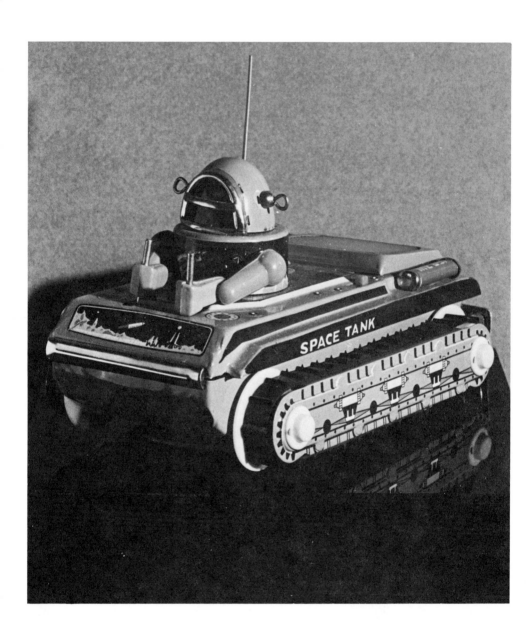

236

To Lt. Calley, Soldier—Vietnam War.

THE GUILT OF A SOLDIER

Through each time of life
Each experiences the right and
    wrong of man
Yet who is
To decide
The guilt of a child
Who is now a soldier?

His world stops
His thoughts are inveigled
His freedom of love stops!
This man, the guilt of a soldier.

Taught to kill
Beyond a word
With freedom at its door
Is this the way of God
Or the way of the world?

Do as I teach
But if too many question
Then you did wrong, my soldier!
You are alone.
We don't know you
Or respect you.

You did what we taught
Now, left alone,
We are afraid
That the guilt of a soldier
Is ours

The reflections in the mirror show only us,
Yet, the blame and scarlet letter is
    on you, my soldier.
'Tis Sad!!

A March 31st I will never forget.

THE BETRAYERS

The day was calm and still
With the appearance of quiet.
The bird's song soon to be sung
Yet, vultures were waiting,
Ready to pick and eat their prey
Why this tragedy of a day?
Suddenly, without warning,
As at the Last Supper
Or at the Roman time of Brutus,
They attacked.
This band of five
With only one thing in mind—
To destroy
Someone.
Not his person
Rather his mind, his ideals

Each had been brought into this man's fold.
Sometimes they helped him,
Comforted him,
Were upset with him.
But never disliked or hurt him—
From some there was love,
Or, so he believed

The first of the conspirators
an evil man
with a forked tongue and crooked plans.
What a lonely man he is,
His intelligence directed to destruction.
His heart not allowing forgiveness for anyone
    or anything
What can such a man be in the eyes of God?

The second of the conspirators
A gambler
Living for the toss and plunge.
His rules are his, alone.
Never understanding rules, regulations or society
Jovial and kind at times
His dreams are only of money and party
Oh, what a disappointment of a man!

239

(continued)

The third and fourth conspirators
are "Men of God"
It is hard to believe they could
Fancy themselves part of such
As they are taught to turn the other cheek
It is a cry of horror
A nightmare of despair
That these two should be part of this
Loneliest of days.

The fifth conspirator
Is part of my life and blood
He was like my brother,
a part of my ever day, my family.
As was his beloved departed wife
His lovely house by the lake
Oh such a disappointment
Oh, such a horror!
He is gone, like the wind-blown
    leaves from a tree
Never to return
A tragedy my family and I
Will never forget,
Never recover from
A bitter sorrow,
Never to be forgotten
That tragedy of a day.

I hope I can trust myself
since all these conspirators
doubt me
I hope I can make allowances
for their doubting
and their lies.
I will not deal in lies
or in hatred.
I won't give way to hating.
They are the pitiful ones,
the sorrowful ones.
I did not hate nor wish bad times for them.
I am truly sorry—
Sorry for their having to remember what they did.

TO BE A JEW

I never knew what that meant,
Yet so many sacrificed their lives for it
Why?
Is there an answer
Or, are the answers only in the wind
Caressed by God?

The heritage of the days of the Old Testament
Yet, it is more than that
These people care
Always wanting to strive ahead
Bearing these fruits of labor
Everknowing the reward is in itself.

The people of being a Jew
have one nose
two eyes
laugh and cry
Yet, they are different only in the
tradition of time
We all believe in one God
One being—Yet to be a Jew
Is a privilege, a need
A Thank-you to God.

There are wrongs and rights for everyone
There are pleasant days
and sad ones
Yet, the Jew has endured all
And is ever striving to succeed in life
Having his place in destiny
And with God

To be a Jew is
To be a human being
Caring
Wanting
Loving and crying
To say "Shalom" is a gift
A gift only given by God.

241

WHAT IS A WOMAN?

Questions of life
Many try to discover
This one has never been unfolded.

Unknown
Undiscovered
Whims, desires
Such happenings,
This is a question;—Woman

Days will pass
Many will adore them,
For their touch
Their fragrant smell
Their closeness
Their warm bodies next to yours
But one question, What is woman?

WHAT IS IT ALL ABOUT?

A stone
A tear
A piece of wood
Life!!!

The hardness of it.
A mood of the world
A way of man
Untold mysteries.

For what!
To ask
To find,
"What is it all about"?

THE PICTURE OF LIFE

Thinking of my life
What I have accomplished
Have I done what others expect
Or have I done what I expect?

Winter comes
And closes us indoors
But few escape to the beauty
    of nature's white rhapsody

Then, the melting of the frost
And the blossom of nature's best
The awakening without effort of
    flower's breast
Rainbows of flowers
    escape into life
Their happenings of life are
    known to all
Yet the picture of your
    life is not short
It becomes small
    only if you so intend
Years are not a yardstick
What have you done?
Have you given yourself
Have you given your love
Have you given joy?

Stop now
You have lived for longer years

For you have given song
Spirit
And yourself
To life

The years have only smiles
And desire

The minutes have strength of
hours

The hours you have given
    will always endure
Into years

You are the reflection of life
Life is you
The years together
Never counted
Only shared
Are not forgotten

The word life
Has one meaning
That is you
For what you are to
    me, my life.

I GIVE THANKS

I give thanks to you
for being what you are to me.
Your caring ways,
your small talk
reaching into my thoughts,
capturing my every whim.
To this, for you,
I give thanks.

For your eyes touching mine,
and only having views for me.
Your nose having the sense of life
for me, just me.
Your aroma is that of fresh new dawn,
with its smell of warm love.
For this I thank you,
love you,
adore you,
want you,
need you,
better than life itself.
To this I give thanks.

WHAT IS A CARD?

This day of yours
Is pulled out of the
    calendar
Especially for you.
Everybody says and
    does things
Just for you.

The difference in this day
    for me
Is that I feel for
and want you
every day
Not just for this day.

When the cards
    come to you
I say, what is in a card?
It is because of you
that this day, as each day of the year,
Gives my heart
an extra beat
And the love of my life
is because of what you do or
say to me.
You mean more than
life itself.

I'M COMING HOME

In the days of my life
I travel
to many different places
Seeing new faces
new smiles
and new tears.
The atmosphere changes
but the pages of the book
   are the same.

There is but one time
Once choice of my life
To know I'm coming home.

This place, home
is the castle of life
the den of love
the foundation of youth
the cure for ugliness and sickness.

I must, I need
my place,
my home,
its community to be known
To have its envelope deliver
my thoughts and needs.
No hostile thoughts
No stopping or needing
   anything or anyone
Except home
For I am coming home
Coming home to you and ours
And the thoughts of only
   you and peace.

WHAT I WANT

I look up to the sky
and see the bluest day
Oh such a day
do I want

I have what you would and
    many want
Yet, is this what I would want?
To thank God
for such gifts
The jewel of life
my love
my loves
The gift of health, above all gems
Yet dubious
Yet such quandary??

For what I want!
I do not know
To ask
To hope
To know
Is only God's gift.

The world I live in
Demands much
Asks much
Wants much
It has taken much from me
Is this what I want?

My face on my children
my love conquering my wife
My home, is me.
But, Oh such a But!!

Many feel this way
The thin road of life
Afraid to front it.
I have loved and will always love,
And have been loved dearly.
Yet what do I want?

I ask do I desire fame
Money
Jewels
Acclaim
Or, peace of mind
To me, what is peace to my mind .
Maybe I will never find it.
But, what I have, God and myself
   will help me.
!

SHADOWS OF YOUR LIFE

We all look back
And see what we could have been.
And ask ourselves, why not me.

Is life so cruel,
So hard?

Or is it soft
as rain drops
or kisses in the night?

Life is what you make.
Take without giving
And the shadows of despair
will appear.

But walk in line
with life
And it will caress you.
Give of yourself
and shadows of your life
will disappear and create
a picture of love
For its beauty is overpowering
its warmth so endearing
All this for just you.

I'VE GOT TO BE WHAT I AM

Each day of my life
I consider why
I do things that many
are amazed at.

I look in the mirror
and see the reflections of life, what
I've got to be, what I am.

Good to my body
but best of all
good to the sky,
the earth and all its people.
Oh, such lovely people
the people of life. They make me
what I am. That is why
I've got to be, what I am.

WHY DID IT HAPPEN?

My study of life
With its branches
its ladders to the sky
its pathways of hidden knowledge.
Be fearful of the winds
that beat you
knock you down
The shadows that bring you to tears
Your teeth grinding
Your heart galloping
Look in the faces of many and ask
Why, oh why,
Did it happen this way?

To my late brother-in-law, Lawrence Schnuer

HEAVEN ONLY KNOWS

This was his year of depression
not a momentary feeling
but a state of mind.
He had all to live for
but a devastating feeling
of self-defeat made him
a loser
A loser of personal and public ego.
Oh, heaven only knows why.

A master in his profession
Yet, like a storm
destroying without reason,
He was destroyed from within
For he always wanted to be
"top banana"
Whatever it took
Losing was inconceivable, intolerable.
Oh, heaven only knows why.

Nobody judged him
except himself.
If victories outweighed defeat,
Nobody counted his winnings
except himself.
All admired him
as he climbed the ladder
of life's achievements,
except himself.
Never enough.
Oh, heaven only knows why.

His true respectful, family
loved him to life's end
And, still, although God has taken
him from earthly being
His work
His desires
were there.
His family, only
wanted this person, him
and only him.
Heaven only knows why.

And this was not good enough
for him.
The power of money
The power of having the American Dream
his family never needed these.
They needed him,
his love,
his being,
And heaven knows why.

Slowly, slowly
he sank into a bottomless pit
trying to revive his life
trying to recover
from the agony of life
and all his ego's
Grasping
Reaching
Yet defeat was his only reward
And shame for believing
was too much for his soul
Heaven knows why.

Now, all is over
There is sorrow for the birds
And despair for his family
And his friends.
His job is no longer his enemy
All is silence
All is no longer
Long or short the dialogue
is just words
The darkness has won
over the daylight
Heaven knows why.

Heaven only knows
why such a happening occurred
The cause and effect is over
As I write, I ask
Dear God in heaven
be gentle with him.

(continued)

He leaves so much behind,
his dear lovely wife
and cherished children
They will always love him
for what he was
not what he wanted to be.

TOO TIRED TO SLEEP

The darkness of the day surrounds my room
The room is quiet.
No signs of life are present—
My eyes and body are too tired for sleep.
My hands are tight with fear,
My fingers tired for want of rest,
My mouth dry and tense;
The only appearance is the want of sleep.
The blue sheet on the bed is a rough sea.
My firm grip around my pillow is my only comfort.
Its warmth and firmness conquers me.
For sleep is but a word.
The darkness crowds in with each sparing moment;
It is all about, and the want for light is gone.
From darkness peace has yet to come,
A world of silence and loneliness.
My eyes are tired and heavy from despair
For sign of relief is nil.
A weary and troubled person can not sleep.
My eyes slowly close.

TO HATE

To provide life
with joy
contentment and
honor with respect,
is what all create and desire
Yet the shadows
of hate appear and deem to conquer.

What is it?
Why?
Does it travel
and spread
Like a broken jar of jam
on smooth clear surface
Is hate a part of life?
Many force it on us.

To have a supposed friend or friends.
To give him or them yourself
With each morsel of breath
With each sign of love
With each desire of contentment

With the ferment of life
your only desire for them

They snap it like a twig
for life is gone
They have broken your hope for everlasting
    friendship
It is but a word to them
But, lifes staff to you!
They invaded you
Pursued you
Harassed you, with ugly dirty talk
Their smiles of contentment
Sincerity is not a word to them.
To contain hurt, is their
    conquest

They have no honor
no joy
no love
and above all
HATE

I PUT THE DAY AWAY

Each day we awake
To a day of hoping
For a day of smiles and cheers
Frowns and despair we wipe
    from our brow to chase it away
Ever wanting
Ever needing
A day of life
Never to be erased from our
    minds or eyes.
This day we want and need.

Such a day
We are hungry for
Need
And desire.
Yet, there are days
Of mishap, of needless talk,
Dark middays and light midnights.
Each mishap is the world's end
Each tear is the flood of the century
Each minute is endless
Each desire is despair.
This day I put away
Hoping that tomorrow will
    bring with the unknown a new light.

THE TIME OF YOUR LIFE

This is the time of your life
When the shadows fall
And the light goes dim
With each gust for
Lust for life,
It can only give you
What you feel
Never judging or asking
The time of your life.

259

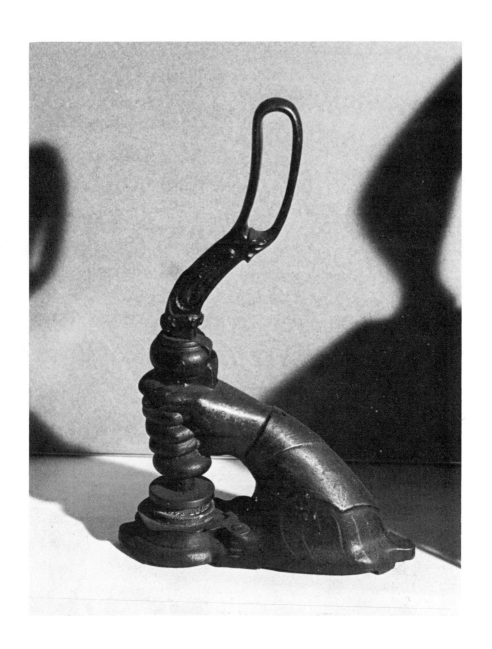

FORGET HIM NOT

Each day of our lives
We all take happenings for granted.
The minutes pass into hours
The weeks into months
As life should be lived on a day to day basis

Never knowing what tomorrow will bring

We forget all the bad
and ask our mind to remember only the sunshine
Glowing upon us and our dear ones.

Yet there is no verse
or march to the beat
When that day comes to say
A life well done.
Accept it because it is of living
Death is a part of life.

We must all try and hunger to achieve one thing.

The feeling that our dear one
Will never be forgotten
His greatest achievement is his
Image on your face and the warmth
you inherited from him

Try to seek
Try to have
Try to be
A gift of life
Forget him not.

IN FAITH

In faith, we believe
In faith, we love
In faith, in our being
In faith in you

The times are now
for strength
for love
for patience
for faith

It will pass
You will endure
for you are life
love
and charm

Whatever may be
We are with you
Your friends, your love
your God
Please believe
In faith, in you.

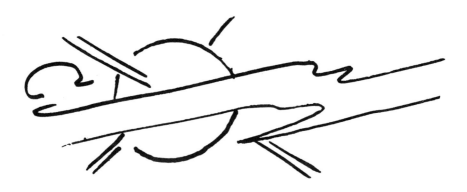

TILL SOON

Each day of our life
We, as a family, ask
That we always be together
Even when
Miles and time lie between us

Raindrops fall
Clear the air with freshness
For all to feel and see
Our love is
Like this wonder of renewal
And soon we shall be
A family united again

The power of our lover for each other
Enriches all who touch our lives
Today's dreams
Will always be tomorrow's memories

We hear the music of love
Across the land and seas
Its vibration never as strong
As our bond for each other
The cord of live with love shall bind us
This year
This day
This hour
This minute
And forever

Till next we all shall meet
And may it be sooner
We shall always remember
That we have each other
To love
To want
To touch
To hold
Then it shall always be till soon
That we shall meet

NOTHING IS FOREVER

Each time we ask ourselves
Was this worth it
Did we have to do it
I tried
I gave so much.
Yet, the end result is
Nothing is forever.

The Time of Man
Looking for his Fountain of Youth
In perpetuity of Life
Yet, nothing is forever.

A blissful marriage
Where two try to love and honor each other
Respect and adore each other.
This true happening can be forever
But is rare and hard to achieve.

One says I gave so much
    to that person
I involved myself with others for them
I jeopardized everything for them
Now look and see and hear
    what the results are
Yet, nothing is forever.

When circumstances occur
One must ask oneself
Are they worth it?
the heartache
the painful sorrow
the aggregation in one's bottomless pit of a
    stomach.

No, for they have no heart
no feeling
no understanding
no loyalty
They forget the past

All you did!
All the struggle and timelss suffering
lack of money
never compromising
they're better gone.

But one must remember
There is something that is forever—
The loyalty and honor of man
Of which they have none.

NOTHING DIES THAT IS REMEMBERED

To look at your smile
your loving face
caressing me and my years
this will never die
so long as it is remembered

As God gave us life
and the seven days
to make what we have
this will never die
because it is remembered

Dear God
we all respect
the wills of men and women
the love of life
the touch of water to one's face
the laugh and cries of life
the smell of fresh cut grass
the sound of sweet and red hot rock n' roll
this too will live on
because
Nothing dies that is remembered!

Letter from Jackie Mason

Bert Padell is not only my dear friend, but he also happens to be my accountant. I always thought of him as a great accountant--especially when I read his poems. There is a close connection between his accounting and his poems, because no one can account for his poems except him. I say this with a great deal of respect because I notice his poems have an exceptional balance-- they balance a lot better than his books. With deep sincerity, I really feel this is the finest book of poetry ever written. The fact that I got a free copy has nothing to do with it.

With Love!

Jack Mason

THE MAN

In our life
we applaud many an entertainer
We laugh at their jokes,
we cry to their capturing charm,
our ears mellow to their music,
This I hear and saw with my body,
    heart and soul.
This was a Man.

A man not of great height
or build,
but a tall branch on a tree.
The strongest of them all.
Its firmness, never afraid
    to bend with the wind.
His face coarse in spots,
yet, smoothness
to one's eyes.

The manner of approach
his own,
never copied or rehearsed
Tis true, it's only he.
Only he when he walks with you.
Only he when he sings to you.
Only he the legend of a man.

For he has divided his life for us
Some have hated this self-centered man,
But this hate could only be jealousy.
For all his bad
The blackboard
has the written word
speaking
of the worthiness of this man;
the warmth,
the childishness he never lost,
his daring love for life
all acts of him
This is a man, one may never
meet or feel in one's life.

This colossus
of flesh and blood
never, never
one hopes and prays
to have a breathless day.
He is a Man, that
God created only once,
this Man

Oh such a treat of life to have him in perpetuity
Love that he gave us that we all caressed from him.

HAVE YOU LIVED

This day is quite different
You have gained a year on life.
Many say, you are closed to the grasp of death,
Others say, you shall begin to become a part of
    life.
Have you seen the pleasant plain of the sea?
While on the other side the tempest of the
    ominous night.
Have you seen the salient men of the world?
While on the other side its knaves and harmful
    hurt.
Have you seen the laughter of a child when a
    dog caresses it with a kiss?
While on the other side its tears of sorrow
    when its love destroys.
Have you seen the love in a man's eyes to find
    his woman of life?
While on the other side the denial by the mate.
Have you seen the first born delight?
While on the other side thoughts of this world
    and its turmoil.
There is much in life.
To touch -- to be a part of,
To worship -- to sin.
All these should be with you.
If not -- make it so.
Life is what you make it.
One gets one chance.
Take it.
Then you can say "I have lived".

TO LOVE

All through the world
And all through life
All want
And desire
The wanting of love.

Oh, such a word--
A dearing sound
A feeling
of warmth.
A feeling of belonging
Companionship,
Knowing, never to be alone
The wanting of love.

How does one capture this
feeling of love?
Is it inherited,
or does one have to earn it,
Work for it,
Struggle to achieve it,
this wanting of love?

It can't be purchased
or received by a special bargain.
One must feel it.
Want it, and desire it above all life's gifts,
This wanting of love.
To love
is to live
To have every day become a new life,
A new desire.
A new happening,
An awakening.

To love
is no task.
It is a beginning.
A start
For all to see
this wanting of love.
Not to be dubious
But granite
With each breath of life within
To know that your love
is my love
To life itself.

Letter from Bert's children

Dear Bert,

The many thoughts you express in this book will touch the heart and soul of those who share your sensitivities and genuine love for all that life holds. We know that all who read it will see your image as the thoughts come off the page that could be those of no other person except Bert Padell.

As the fortunate ones who are able to call you family we want to tell you first how very much we love you and how proud we are to be your loved ones. When the readers turn the pages and grow to know you better and see your kindness, generosity and love they might only wonder how it feels to be part of your family. We need not guess as we know how wonderful it is.

We thank you for all that you have given us in life, we respect you for all that you have accomplished, but most of all we love you for all that you are.

Bobby,
Ellie, Scott, Wendy
David & Randi

Letter from Fonzi Thornton

When I think of Bert Padell- I have to smile. In all the years I've been a client of his, I always admired how much he is admired by others and now I know why. In a business where friends come and go, he has proven to be the genuine article. I've never been to him with a problem that he didn't shed some serious light on. His advice is always wise and never condescending. This is man that really cares about people, so he is very easy to care about. He has encouraged, and supported right from the first, he knows how to be impartial and yet he is the best person to have on your side when the going gets tough. Bert, thanks for sticking with me, you can bet I'll be sticking with you -

Love
—Fonzi Thornton

HOW DOES ONE FEEL FOR LIFE

Each morning the sun rises
and we waken to a new life.
For some,
short and sweet.
For others, dark and despair.
We cannot control these happenings,
ever hoping
that tomorrow will bring today's dreams.

Yet
we all have to pay the price
for our doings in life,
Our feelings,
our hopes.
Life's happenings we weather
for its fruits,
Many never achieving the taste
of sweet life.
The few that do
Touch the softness of her lips,
her smooth, warm embrace
Caressing your body ever more.
This feeling, this hoping it will never end
This desire for more and more...

Your eyes darken, opening for the sight of
her face reflecting yours.
This is how one feels
for the rhapsody of life.

BELIEVE IT

A Christmas day comes to all
With its presents and joyful glare
The young and old are one,
To make a holiday of warmth.
As the day comes forward,
Joy and despair are present.
All thank God; and ask for good health,
    and a better life.
If all mankind could leave its ominous
    fear of each other,
This day I do believe would be a sign of God.

IT NEVER STOPS

As I look
I wonder
Its sound
strong and crushing
with each ruffle
its conflict
always there
because in all that lives
conflicts must be.

Its roar
pleasing to some,
striking to others
Many walk through
its sound
an everlasting sound.
touching
Inveigling and capturing
your feelings and wants.

This day I saw a set of four
walking upon the sand
this ocean of water
never stopping
always having
the same script.
Never the same audience
They, free from the world's troubles
Their mind clean
wanting each other.
fresh air
conquering them
love was present captivating all.

WHAT I ASK OF YOU

Each one of us
lives through life
never touching
or finding
the one aspect of life,
   you.

Each of us has thoughts,
some true
many fascinating.
We try to live in a world
  of make believe,
This never happening.

For us to find true
   thoughts
true believing in oneself
and ever seeking, finding,
a person, a being, that one
can confide in,
Talk to, Having a strong subtle ear,
Never deaf
or offensive.

This is what I ask of you.
No one hears my thoughts
my joys
my sorrows
my tears
my ever wanting
desire for freedom,
Only you, dear love.

What I ask of you is
to listen
and help,
not for just a thought
but for love
of letting my
body release
energies,
worries, desires
to you, I ask!
This is what I want of you,
my dear friend, and dear love.

PRECIOUS LOVE

The precious item of life
is love.
To be loved and to love
is the aroma of sweet honey,
Fresh water and rain after the cutting
    of grass,
The softness of a baby's cheek
The warmth of your love's body,
Touching, embracing, tingling,
    intercoursed with yours.
Life is dear and sweet
though greater than the diamond stone,
Stronger than the rock,
Coarser than the sea,
More handsome than the rainbow.
Taste the aroma of a clear spring day
Strong as a child's love for her mother.
These items of life
Are items of human want.
He or she is what they are,
no better or worse
For what they have done.
Yet what they have done is what they are.

GIVE THANKS

I look around
To see what I have.
Bottomless I'm not
Thankful for much.

God has given me
A part of the sky,
   with its clear magnificent pad of columns
Light to have me feel and want
   its glorious wonders.

I need not see to feel
   parts of nature
With its touch of winter awakening
   into spring
and have hot summer move into tinted autumn.

What I have, man might want more or less.
All of us made from the same seed,
Yet bloom in different directions.

I thank thee for choices I can give,
The thoughts I can have
and feelings I can endure.
For this, I give thanks.

WHAT IS A WOMAN?

Questions of life
Many try to discover
This one has never been unfolded.

Unknown
Undiscovered
Whims, desires
Such happenings,
This is a question; -- Woman

Days will pass
Many will adore them,
For their touch
Their frgrant smell
Their closeness
Their warm bodies next to yours
But one question, What is woman?

To watch their lazy smiles
Afraid to take it
As carelessness to the heart

or just the evasive way of a woman
Such charm when, they want, or desire
Is this woman?

To make love
Silence in nature, yet her smell whimpers
    your body
Her hand caresses your body
Her body firm and strong
Which only makes you stronger and desirous
Your lips touch hers and darkness captures you.
Your body intertwined with hers
Fulfilling all emotions
Oh, such a wanting.

For this woman
At her greatest moment
A master to none
Loving and wanting,
She has made, asked
and known -- That she is woman.

For all to Know:

Bert is very unique. He's that special advise I always need. He's that quiet wonderful man that always has time to talk to me, whether baking delicious brownies or talking to the largest accounts. He is a friend, when your down will be there before you ask.

Humanitarian, he was one before it was cool! The man that started out a bat boy in New York has been hitting home runs as long as I have known him.

From my family + me, who pulls no punches we love you deeply.

Keep Kicking them out!

Rowdy Roddy Piper '88

Florence, June 3rd 1988

Dear Bert,

" I shall never get you put together entirely
Pieced, glued and properly jointed!..."
Indeed, thinking about you, Bert
these lines of Sylvia Plath's
poem "The Colossus," seem to
discribe quite well how I feel about
you: Bert, the immensly successful
Businessman, the sportsman,
the collector, the excellent
"patissier," who bakes cakes for
his friends, and last not least
the poet, the artist, well I guess,
thats where we always connected
and understood each other
from my first days in New-York,
where we somehow
started together.

Don't forget, keep in touch,
as you always say.

Love Verushka

A SUMMER END

The swiftness of a rain cloud did our
   summer end.
Our memories shall be tenacious
The hours move uncounted if fun or sorrow
   had occupied its presence.
The smile and tears of weather are present.
God's sun lifted many out of their city-smoked
   shell.
It cleared the dirt from the youth's face.
Brightening the gleam that only happiness can
   endure.
Life became bearable, tasteful and romantic.

Harmony seen from the trees,
Caressing the lakes.
Evening stillness capturing the darkness of night.
Yet the summer will pass,
And all the beauty will enchant our mind.

One never forgets hurt and ugliness,
But the superbness of summer,
Will enhance mind and soul.
A magnificent rhapsody of love
Has tip-toed into our hearts,
And has made this summer
A summer of summers.

TO THE ARMS OF MY WORK

One always asks
Without that
I just couldn't
Exist.
The sky might not be blue
The air, polluted as it is,
The noisy street tingling and raging
The screech of the voice of man,
These are part of our every day.

One thing is for sure
Without each of you
My life would not be what it is
Your dear help, assistance, are
my hands and my love
Your talk is mine
Your laughter I feel.
Your frown and/or sweet smile
Have the reflections of me.
You all are my arms.
Without the arms and heart I am waste.
Humbly I can only say
"Thank you" for
A job you have all performed.

ODE TO ALLEN

The laughter of many he did conquer
A tear of thoughtfulness did prevail.
His wit and humor as that of an Arizona day.
God has taken his hand to lead the show.
Should we remember such an astute showman as he?
His face coarse and ugly
The rings around his eyes, only to show worry and heartache.
A voice deep and strong,
To carry way across the oceans.
His size not of a giant, but of a man.
We the world have lost him
To a greater being of all.
His performances will be few,
But spectacular if any.
An audience he shall have, far greater than ever before.
A farmer
An executive,
A professional man,
An artist,
God.
Will all sit and judge.
He need not fret,
For the joy, and contentment he has brought
Will least not be forgotten.
God brought him into the world of being
He so taketh away.
Yet his memory will blot our thoughts forever and a day.

HER LITTLE RED SHOES

When I first heard,
I wondered what it was.
Its sound was gentle,
quiet to my hearing,
pleasant and
caressing to my mind.
Its color a horizon of bright red,
the size, oh so tiny,
So petite,
so cuddly,
caressing her soft delightful feet.
Oh, they were a sight to be seen.
She was so loveable on her toes,
    always showing off
    her little red dancing shoes.

"SORRY"

Many for the sake
of the spoken word
Would say "Sorry"
For this happening
For their sorrow
Yet the work blank to my hearing

Time can care for us all
Yet times wait for some
Never moves.
The wanting for just a minute
Never arrives
Time
Never to pass

Your sorrow
Seen
Felt!
Never wanted
Afraid!
Trying to escape it
Undeserving, yet there.
No one wants
Or wishes
Desires
Sorrowful thoughts.

One cannot replace them
Exchange
Misuse
Thoughts of man
By just saying, "Sorry."

The heart
has a tear
A sigh
A wishful thought
of only you -- the grief

An exchange
You to me
The second -- word of
    "Sorry"

THE SHADOW HAS PASSED

The ways of the world
Move in different directions.
For some, good is bad
and bad good -
Yet have we not all wronged?
To wrong is not a sin
It is the intention of man to
govern.

A shadow appeared very still
It could be seen
But not with the human eye
It convinced us all, never let up.
Oh such pain and toil
for what?
Why?

Now this shadow has commonly appeared
Its ugly hands always
knowing
Yes, my man has wronged.
He said tales, that were false.
Yes, we all have done this.
But, he is our leader, our number one.
From this happening, may the
shadow of doubt, deceit,
horror pass from him and us all
and change us all
to start anew, in a place where shadows
are just words of no meaning or seeing
but that of the past.

TIME

Each day that opens
Has a smile or a frown
Oh, for such a happy day
To know time will pass
and I will be there.
The fragrant movement of life
Is a rhapsody to itself

Times moves, and waits for no one
With no feelings
Or excuses, or cares
Just time!!

WHY NOT!

I've dreamed of the prettiest
I've dreamed just to dream
Yet most of us
Dream of things.
They never happen!
Yet we continue,
And
Say
Why not!!

I LIVE TODAY

I see many contented with life
Yet they worry for tomorrow
Afraid of what life may offer them.
Security is the biggest asset they
    hunger for.
To meet the onslaught of competition they
    quaver.
They appall the air of firmness.
Yet as I might be harassed by many
Or have an ominous fear of life itself,
I live for today.
And what must be for tomorrow, will be!

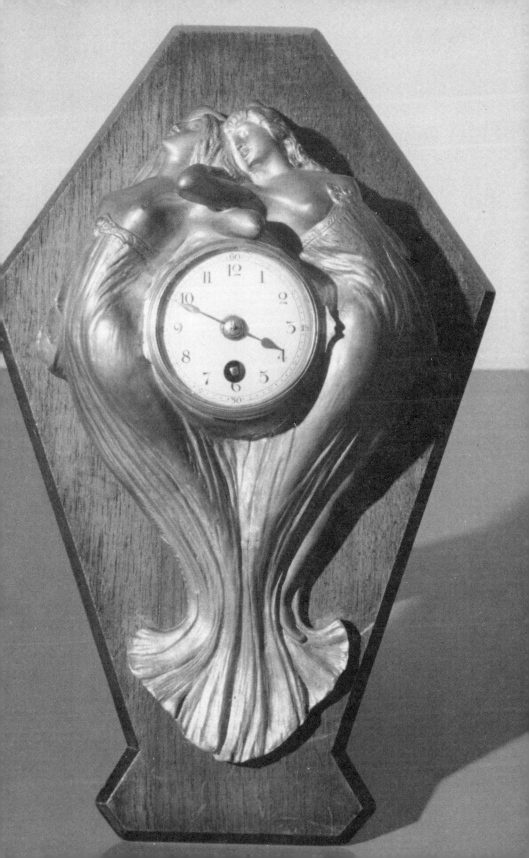

ONE YEAR OLDER

This day like many --
Its hours and movements seem no different
    than any other.
Yet my close and dearest friend
Has moved up on life by one year.
He feels no different than yesterday,
His ways of life have not transcended
    from him.
Tears he has shed will still be no
    stranger,
Love and laughter will always be his
    close partners.
And yet today he is one year older.

WHEN WE GROW UP

When the years pass,
we all wonder
asking ourselves
Which of the "Seasons" we love,
oh, so much.

The one I love and cherish
for all of us
to see and live by,
is Christmas.

Its season
its smell of love
fairplay and warmth.
It allows us, the grown ups,
to be children once again,
    and be young.

THE MEETING OF STRANGERS

I never looked at your eyes.
Your face questions me.
Is your hair brown?
The voice you speak enchants me;
The time will come when we shall meet.

THE TIME OF YOUR LIFE

As I wait for the time of life
I wonder,
The waiting for the sunrise
The freshness of its start
The slowness of its end
The light it brings, declaring to many
Yet darkness!
Is this the time of your life?
Is it the aroma, sweetness of a woman's night?
Is it the crackle of lover's talk?
Is it the love of heaven's firmament?
Is it the freshness of a baby's cry?
Is it when you reach your bottomless walk?
Or when you reach to the sky for the time of your life.
For too many -- money is the time of your life.
To others the sweetness of you.
The kiss of night,
The warmth of her cheek,
The tingle of her breath near you,
The roar of the gun,
The want of despair
The wanting to hate
The love of love
Are these the time of your life?
Finding the answers why?
Is this the time of your life?
From the answer itself,
You have found,
Why, What and Life.

© The Walt Disney Company

Recording Studios

EDWARD GERMANO
President

BERT PADELL

Who is Bert Padell?

A kind, sensitive, compassionate, loving friend.

Always a friend.

Ed Germano

Letter from Little Steven

Life, generally speaking, is a war.
Good moments are rare - good things rarer still.
Most of our time is spent as soldiers
fighting a war we didn't ask for or create
fighting for a clean environment
fighting for homes for the homeless
fighting to stop crime in the streets
fighting to stop crime in our government
fighting to stop treaty violations of the Native American
    Indians
fighting for peace in Latin America
fighting for peace in the Middle East
fighting for democracy in South Africa
fighting for respect for our elderly
fighting for women's rights
fighting for children's rights
fighting for education
fighting for animals' rights
fighting to keep our bills paid
fighting our own insecurities
fighting our own ignorance
fighting our own prejudices
fighting our own loneliness.
Every once in awhile, if we work hard enough and
    look hard enough, we stumble into a good thing, and
    that's what keeps us going.
My wife is one of those good things.
My dog is one of those good things.
My family is one of those good things.
Calling Bert Padell my friend is one of those
    good things.

                        Little Steven

A PUZZLEMENT OF LIFE

My life a printed page in a book,
Some bad impressions, some favorable.
The writing is clear,
Yet my eyes cannot bear the smallness of the
    print.
My heart is silent,
But life is still wild and full of its
    mystic force.
My thoughts transcend time,
Why is this?
The wind outside is coarse,
The branches on the trees make ready for
    the rape of spring,
The puffy clouds of heaven surround my thoughts.
These sparks of life are sealed within my breast
If only to have my thoughts alive.
To have my den of darkness brought to light,
And to have the echoes of man tell me,
That the pieces of the puzzle are all in place.

THE TIME WILL COME

As each day passes
My thoughts are of you
The many enchanting hours coupled with
    love and tears.
Now dissolved for many cruel months,
Not cruel in meaning but lonely in thought.

Winter will approach,
With its milky clouds of cold
A breath of smoke to define the cold.
The black of night, to only have
Winter depart into mirror picture spring.

Our time for sight together is on the threshold.
Spring will make life more bearable to live until
    we shall meet.
Victories of the flowers bloom
Its sprinkle of life and colored beauty
Its fragrant aroma of sleeping trees and flowers.

All this shall pass from my mind.
My feelings shall vanish
Only to know,
The time will come, when you, and I shall meet.

YOU ARE YOUR OWN

Each of us wants to be
    our own person.
But what is that to you?
Does the sky have to touch
    your ego?
Are these material benefits of life
    gathering at your feet,
Or is there something different for you?

When I first saw your eyes,
They told me with their hazel touch,
That you wanted the fruits of life
But, your own,
Your mountain of thoughts
desires
loves
happen with time.

Never stop your emotions
They are you.
When that day occurred,
Your heart had its extra strike
of wanting and knowing
You are your own lady
With your mind
and body.
You shall achieve
your own
and from there
You shall find
A love greater than ever
    you have experienced.
And most tingling,
when his touch caresses yours,
    and only then
Will you be your own, as a woman!

GOD SITS ON HIS PILLOW

The seasons of the year
are pleasures of my mind.
God has given them to me
To caress, to fulfill my desires and whims.
Through the fortune of life
I have found
A man of all seasons.

There was a man who came into my life
A sort of fellow
One might not meet everyday
His gentle manner
God's touch.
His special love of family
Gave me waves of warmth
for there never was despair
in his thoughts or desires
only love and contentment,
This man of all seasons.

His love for the young
never turing a deaf ear,
never a cold cheek
Always an expression of love and hope
to them.
Always willing to have patience
with them.

A companion to one and all,
He would walk in riches
And never lose the common touch
This man of reason, of all seasons.

God always set on his pillow
to rest and know
that this man had done his job
well
for his life,
his family, for his friends

Now, God, sitting on his pillow,
has called him
as a call in need.
We all cry
and ask but why?
But, we all know
he is needed
and going to a greater being.

We have learned through him
And will always need him
but, he is always with us all.
God has said, he will always
sit on our pillows each day of our lives.

THE ROUND TABLE OF PEACE

Many sit before a great table to decide the makings of the
    world;
Their wisdom echoes over people of all creeds.
The mirror-picture of kindness and peace; from
    Moses and Christ
For all to adhere to.
May their tender feelings be spoken at this table;
The word of peace is here; may the reality of this prevail.

THE LUST FOR WAR

Time for prosperity seems to be only in war.
The wickedness of people's minds do prevail this thought.
Peace and prosperity are brothers to all,
Vengeance and greed make enemies of this.
To have love for man sow its seed,
Lust for war would be just a word.

SILVERBERG, ROSEN, LEON & BEHR
A PARTNERSHIP INCLUDING PROFESSIONAL CORPORATIONS

June 7, 1988

Mr. Bert Padell
1775 Broadway
New York, New York 10019

Dear Bert:

I cannot tell you how much I enjoyed our meeting in New York. Everyone I know who knows you speaks so warmly and highly of you that I began to doubt your bona fides. However, they are real. You are a fascinating human being and, more importantly, a very nice one. I regret the years that I did not take advantage of a potential friendship. I promise you not to make that mistake in the future. Please let me know when you are visiting California. You are definitely on my list when I come to New York.

Warmest personal regards,

DAVID A. BRAUN

GRUBMAN INDURSKY & SCHINDLER, P. C.
ATTORNEYS AT LAW

July 18, 1988

Dear Bert,

It is humbling to think of how many years we have known each other. Over this period we have had a mutually beneficial business relationship. But more importantly, we have been friends. Whenever I have needed sincere personal advice I have called upon you and you have been there. You are a compassionate, authentic, truly virtuous man. It is reflected in your poetry.

All my love,

Allen Grubman

MY FRIEND IS GONE

The wisdom of men
The riches of kings
The common places of man
The wanting to help, my friend, it's you.

To live a lifetime,
To have one like you
Is man's greatest gift
The gift of life, my friend it's you.

In time of despair
You die with me
In time of joy we share together
For the coin tolls two sides,
    my friend, it's you.

The rain drops little parts of life
Each one having a task
A sign of life
A chapter in a book,
my friend, it's you.

The page in a book
Adventurous,
Despairing,
Joyful,
Loving,
Each of these you have given to me
my friend, it's you.

For better, for worse,
That is our voice
To know each,
To know our best
To know our weakness,
    my friend, it's you.

You shall never despair me
For you are me
A forked tongue
You shall stop against me
For you are, my friend.

If I shall die
  before my time
I shall know you have
  been with me.
By my side, when ugly knaves haunt me
  You my friend, are you.

What!
It could not be?
They said, you just let it happen
Your talk was theirs,too
But why?

If it were me, there would be no talk.
My friend, is this you?

TWO TO COME

Two months have past,
The flowers still caressing the skies
All love still in bloom
Mountains firm, yet soft next to God's paradise.
The stars twinkle at all who are partners with love
A summer romance has appeared.
Out of sight we are
Conjecture enters our mind and heart,
We now see and touch all parts of life.
Is this "True love" for us alone?
Or are we just inveigled by life's happenings --
That this love of ours shall live forever.
Do we know it was no summer romance?
Days and weeks shall pass bringing us closer together.
Our burning quiet love shall set aflame to brighten our eyes.
Love has made us one for life.

SOON WE WILL BE ONE

It seems as if it were yesterday
That our love found each other.
We never dreamed this could happen,
Two people, two hearts, one love for each other.
Time will pass
To unite us into one.
Moving faster than a sign,
It never waits.
My love for you has grown like a newly planted seed.
Ripening with each day.
Soon we shall be one, my love
Never will it die.
If so, I will love thee after death doth part us.

AFRAID TO BE HURT

When first this happening touched you,
you were oh, so young,
so delicate
so sheltered
from life's small ventures.
Having only in your mind,
Why must I be hurt?

This deed affected many in your life.
The wound is healed,
but the scar tissue is always seen
in your heart
in your desire for love
and contentment.

Why should you
hold back?
Is it recapturing
that same event,
Or, is it that the puzzle has
many of the same pieces and
You wish it were free of puzzlement?

In this way, he would be only yours,
to caress love passionately,
Never afraid to be hurt anymore,
With the endless desire, never to hurt him.

This dream of yours,
When his lips embraced yours
and your body outstretched, tingling
    with supreme desire
Ever hoping that his thoughts and body
    would intermesh with yours.

Oh, such a want
and need.
Yet, this fear
this bereft feeling.
Please,
May it disappear!

If you could walk with him
in this state of love
for a day
a month
Or a moment.
Yet, never to have him for your very own
Still having had all the fruits of love
Your fears would dissipate.

Your wanting him
Would be shared
Oh, look to the sky
and its bridges of white.
You have crossed them,
knowing true love,
and your fear has disappeared.

THE LOSS OF A LOVE

Through the years
Many obtain various
Pleasures and
Heartaches,
but to lose a love like yours is death
   itself.

We had our differences
You liked white I liked black.
You smoked, I abhored it.
A painting on a wall I could feel
You could only see it.

Bad talk from people
Never touched me about you,
It did of me, to you. .
My only thought was to help you
Never to remember what and how I did.
You remembered the bad
The good was very little thought of.

My children had
adopted an uncle
Your warmth entered their heart
Your smile made them feel life
You conquered them
They loved you.

When I was a child
  oh so young,
Oh, to be young so young, to forgive and forget.
But years toll around
We never forget and never forgive.

You were part of me,
To talk to you only.
About my feelings
Yet you spurned it
Didn't want to know
Afraid, to get involved
I would for you
But the coin has two sides
My side falls on tails.

As I see today,
And what I've lost
I say, I've done no wrong.
Hurt you not.
But you have made my
body drag and despair
My thoughts void.
For I have lost a love
which had made me the richest of men
and the king of kings.
Now all is gone, and you are lost.

A-PART

A-Part we must be
To make a vital test,
Our test of love!
Whether it is or not, is our question
Miles separate us
This is our only problem of life
We both say it is for the best
It will test our undying love.
Yet as darkness crowds in, sleep we must
There is none for us.
When hunger enters the body,
Its taste vanishes from our thoughts.
Life is but a word to live by
Not for us --
You and I made it life
Times shall move like a Friday in New York
Only to know that we shall be together.
If only for a fortnight.
Yet in our thoughts the time will come,
When A-part shall just be a mere expression to us,
And together we shall always be.

WHY MUST THIS BE?

As I look out my hazy window,
Pictures appear,
A child crying for his mother; its cry over-shadowed
    by her stentorian tone.
Man and Woman each in love, as time moves on many a
    precarious attitude is unfolded.
Brother and Friend unite into one, but deceit and
    hate seem to conquer.
Must all these ugly knaves appear through my window?
My view is clear, as a brisk morning in winter
But why must life be so unbearable as this?

TILL NEXT WE MEET

The time has come for us to bid farewell,
Strangers we are not; but everlasting friends.
A meeting such as ours should be remembered.
If you can force your love to be strong
Our parting will not seem long.
The autumn leaves will fall, the snow will melt,
The coming of the sparrow, the blossom of the trees,
    the fragrant pines of summer-
All these meaningful God creations, we both love.
Time is but a word, which moves ever so quickly,
And our paths shall meet once more in the friendship of
    our hearts.

THE CURE

Endless years have past; many men have tried to cure the
    unkindness of disease
Their tasks have been hopeful in effort, with only slight
    success.
Through their undying efforts, rays of success have come.
The Maker of all has tried; the people have prayed,
    the stricken have hoped.

SWEET LOVE OF MINE

I look across the field of green
Through the picture mirror of you
To feel the softness of the air
Is the softness of you.
Color blowing me around
  is the sureness of your smile.
Ah, the wind blowing, strong against the
  ruffle of the trees
Is the talk of you, ready and willing
  to caress my every thought.
With all fragrance touching my nostrils
  yours aroused
My inner mind
My body
My every want -- my dearest desire
  for you.
Oh, such sweet dear love
For you and I have
  loved
When oh so young
That, through passing years,
  love
Touches us
And you are love,
  sweet love of mine.

YOUR CHANCE SHALL COME

Thru life we enjoy many gracious experiences
Time makes us endure many unhappy occurrences
Each one must take his own in stride.
Hoping he can hold on --
The going may be rough,
Unbearable to foresee a clear sky.
The will must be there --
The wanting to win,
Makes one head the rest.
To be harassed by many
Ugly knaves knocking at his door,
Yet knowing to turn away on all this
A man must be of thought and will to achieve his life's goal.
Yet your chance shall come,
Take it!
Fear not, for those that fear this will to go ahead,
Will always fear life itself.

TO ASK FOR LOVE

The sun rose today out of its sleepy nest
caressing all its loves
nourishing and demanding
its attention to be faithful and wanting
to mother sun.

As the day moves with each second, a story.
The morning makes ready
for such a day -- and what a day!
Each day a year in itself
A novel to be told,
but such a day for you or I to want.

It is a busy
noiseless affair
many and many are there
with all its movement

Ready for a tear
Applauding a happiness
Crying for a sorrow
A smile for a new life
Everlasting yearning to be loved
It is a better thought
to be loved.
Then never entertaining the thought.

Slowness appears on the scene
for the day, has moved for some
    as a dismal rain
but for others as children on a love-
    spread merry-go-round.

This has been such a day
For love
For wanting
Never let it go
Yet, as life is,
It must fade
into time, yet never lost in memory.

It was asking for love
and did achieve it
for it gave much in return
without love, there is no life -- nothing
God's gift to mankind is the
giving
and accepting
of love.

MY OWN TOWN

Each time I read the newspapers
or listen to the news of the day,
Many complain
and scorn my own town.

Is my town different?
Or is it like many?
Well, my town
with its long sticks reaching into the sky,
and its many lights flicking on and off,
Its sweet aroma of gas and fumes,
Its horror at night,
Afraid to enjoy
the wonders of this great city.
This my own town.

Yet, this is expected
    of all towns, cities and people.
People are what they are
some funny
some coarse
some small
some tall,
but, best of all, the people in my town are people's people.

Oh, such a town,
Its dragons going from borough to borough
    through the ground,
making all arrive on time
for work
for pleasure
and love.

The people of my town are of all kinds,
all colors
all languages,
an education in itself.
They live, work and love
    in this, my town.

My town touches art
with all its glory and energy.
Never a place unturned
    for want of food and drink.

The taste for pleasure
never
lacking
my theatre and any spice of life
Touched at a given notice
This is my town.

This town of mine
Second to none
First in all respects
it gives itself
just for the taking.

Cherish it,
never let it go.
For it is mine and yours
Only for the asking
With her arms open wide,
ready and willing to capture
    all that want her.
I do love my town and treasures.

Bert's words are a song of beauty... the best feelings that life has to offer.

Dear Bert:

I've been an avid admirer of your poetry for many ___ TV and radio seasons. I look forward to introducing your latest book on my shows.

Joe Franklin
WWOR-TV
WOR-AM
4/27/88

TO: BERT PADELL

FROM: PHIL RAMONE

When given the opportunity to tell the truth about someone
else, it conjours up a chance to be salty or schmear the person
in butter. Bert is the most concerned and caring man I have
ever met. Rightfully so, he didn't make it in baseball, as
a musician, actor or philanderer. By the way, nothing wrong
in not being flashy or dishonest. He is so normal and straight
arrow, he decided to dedicate himself to the collection of
crazy thoroughbreds he handles like a Spencer Tracy. He ab-
solutely loves us like his family. He gives me all that the
brother I didn't have would have given. He worries more than
all our mothers. He prays and cries with you. The phone
rings and the soft spoken voice says, "It's Bert, are you
okay?" If I say, "I just jumped off Mt. Kilimanjaro," he
says, "Don't worry, it will be alright. Always think positive!"

In closing , remember, he is Santa Claus, The Cookie Man,
and the guy who made me write this piece so I'll have to buy
the book!

                              Love,
                              Phil Ramone

I KISS MY COUNTRY

The place I live
Is one place
Is one town
Is one State
That is second to none
It has small, large buildings
The sun warms us
The rain wets us
The snow makes us cold
The wind moves us
Just for my Country.

My Country a place to live
A place to grow
The chance given to anyone,
Size, shape, color makes no differnce.
I talk, right or wrong
Opinion?
The alphabet on the board
   the words different from yours,
But, my country -- free, to have a clear head
Unafraid to speak.
My loves can touch me
Such as,
Walking down a street
Striking a match
Sipping a glass of wine
The taste mine, such a taste.
The dirt I touch
is mine
It smells so sweet
Oh so dark
Good Earth!
I walk on it
It caresses me,
Holding me.

For it's free.
Free, from despair
Free from hunger
Free from being afraid
Free for opportunity
Free for wanting, the desire to go ahead.

My belief in God
Strong
Yet the belief in a religion
Born into one.
Not knowing, why, where or what!
This burden on me
Yet I accept it for the birth right
   of my family.
My country lets me think, feel this way.

WHAT DO I WANT

I look up to the sky
and see the bluest day
Oh such a day
do I want

I have what you would and
    many want
Yet, is this what I would want?
To thank God
for such gifts
The jewel of life
my love
my loves
The gift of health, above all gems
Yet dubious
Yet such quandry??

For what I want!
I do not know
To ask
To hope
To know
Is only God's gift.

The world I live in
Demands much
Asks much
Wants much
It has taken much from me
Is this what I want?

My face on my children
my love conquering my wife
My home, is me.
But, Oh such a But!!

Many feel this way
The thin road of life
Afraid to front it.
I have loved and will always love,
And have been loved dearly.
Yet what do I want?

I ask do I desire fame
Money
Jewels
Acclaim
Or, peace of mind
To me, what is peace to my mind
Maybe I will never find it.
but, what I have, God and myself
   will help me.

THE REMEMBRANCE OF A POET

A friend not to me, but to many
The poetry he has written
Brings across a meaning from his heart.
Thoughts of love and despair are found by his pen.

Now, he has died, by the movement of life.
A wan feeling many do have from this.
His writings will be read and loved.
One cannot forget words from the heart.

UNFORGOTTEN DEATH

A day of mourning not seen too often by you;
Your life is sweet, as the aroma of lilacs to
    ones senses
Like the quickness of time
This sudden and unkindly act occurred.

Mourning may be everlasting in your heart.
Tears you have shed will cease with time,
Life today is cold and unkind.
Death has touched your heart; to be a
    memory forever.

LOVE'S END

The caress of love you once had,
Your tender affections you did show,
The tears you have shed are all in vain;
For all is gone of this love.

Songs of the birds are thoughts of precious love,
Seasons of spring unfold many loves.
Your wan and disheartened look, only to vanish;
For lone like you, to find love.

The omniscience of your talk,
Your desire for unselfish love.
To you alone; you must love sincerely and deeply.
As life opens to you I will enter your heart of love.

DON'T TOUCH

Our love for each other
Is just for us to hide.
My love is true and there, only for you.
Yet, time tells me
that you have to wait.
Tis true I can't
   But I do understand
and know that I cannot
   touch your love
Till tomorrow's day.

BEAR FRUITFUL THOUGHTS

Think of me, as badly as you wish
Think of me, and bare your thoughts
For the sinew of life, in your
   thoughts of him.
He, just a man!
Yet such a gentle, timid one.
His efforts
His doings
His thoughts
All, only of you,
Bear fruitful thoughts of the past
Of what has been done.
And what he will do, for you only.
For your thoughts of him now
Can only hurt
destroy
And yet circumstances will never
   justify your doings.
Cast the stone on me
Not on him
And bear only fruitful and endearing
   thoughts of him.

I AM WHAT I AM

Each day I see a face
familiar
Yet a stranger at times
This picture a man
Is me! and oh such a me!
Yet, I am what I am
Many try to forget
To blot out the past
Bottomless boredom
Freshness for excitment
Life for its own sake
Years of inveigled fears
Of a lost horizon!
Yet they are what they are.
On a still calm shiny day
Many are sluggish
Ill-tempered
Wanting only cool rough wetness
Yet the dullness of the heat
Rapes them
Captures all their senses
And marks them as almost dead.
Yet they are what they are.

To the world
This great vast hurtful sphere
Many look at another
And the spoken word is said
To have only what the next has
Never content, what each other has
A need of more
An appetite to get
Never to give
Yet they are what they are.

Each in a little room
To know
To be human, is to err,
Except for some,
And learn to achieve from the mistake.
The poor and the sickly learn
of the mistaken life they lead,
Ever hoping, never to cross the bridge
they are at,
Praying that what they are will soon change.

Letter from Lisa Fischer

Dearest Burt,

You have such a special
gift! I've not known you long
but even the first time we've spoken
I've felt like I've always known you.
I love your warmth. Your wife and
children are lucky to have you.
And thru your poetry we can also
share a part of you!

Love to you
always! Lisa Fischer!

Letter from Art Rust Jr.

7/26/88

If poetry is on your menu...
Berts book is a piece
of filet mignon.
    Its one of the best
of its kind.
        Bert ... your book
is a four base hit.
        Good luck...

        Art Rust Jr.

MY SON, MY SON

The air is still and quiet,
The fragrant smell of flowers are gone.
The world of being seems to cease,
For my son, is lost.
I pray, to ask if this be just.
All men have their way of prayer,
But I have never prayed, or asked for anything
But my son, is lost.
How does one pray?
And ask for his son,
Only to return,
And see his eyes of love.
I ask, only you to hear me.
Have I done wrong, in my life?
Which I cannot ask for repentance.
For my sins, are not my sons.
If one must suffer, the hurt of man
May the burden rest only on me.
For he is cherishable,
And I do love him.
If only the world of being could open its tender eyes.
For man is kind and gentle.
Let all walk with the wind,
And not be perturbed by it,
And my son will be found.

BRING US TOGETHER

My heart moves a little faster
  for my only hope is prayer,
For love, to all of us.
We have been moving in various directions.

Apart
Unaware!

We are only strong together,
Weak if we move alone

Please, I pray
        I beg
        I ask
        I hope!
Bring us together
My beloved country.

A PARTING LOVE

Each leaf that falls to earth,
A tear of thought I feel.
The loveliness it once had is gone.
A dilatory sight shall appear soon.
My thoughts are in a quandry,
To ask why, my autumn leaves fall to earth,
As if to tell me, our love has ceased.

AUCTION OF LIFE

Can I go to my town auction?
To buy, to price, my wonder of life.
There are many fashionable items there
Yet their greatest audience is dust.
The bidding to reincarnate them to life
Yet their voice has no sound
Their love no warmth.
Only beauty to some, and wastefulness to many
One can not buy this wonder of life.
Many over centuries have tried to achieve this goal
Theirs has past, never to return
The ever hoping of a rebirth of youth
To learn by one's mistakes and start again
Letting experience be one's partner
Knowing the greatest treasure of life is life itself.
The challenge to say alive
Ugly knaves knocking at one's door
Sinful fruits to taste
Tearful skies
Nights of quiet
All this one goes to the town auction
To bid for life, to start again; ever hoping the
    gavel won't say "Sold" to another, other than you.

YESTERDAY'S DAY

As early morn surrounded my thoughts,
I realized the day had past never to return
Gone; only the memories
The night was swift and painless,
As if a spear had entered my body and descended
Why did that day pass?
Everything seemed so wonderful.
The hours on the clock pass at my desire,
The sun never hazed my eyes,
My food tasted as sweet as sugar cane,
My drink absorbed my thirst.
All was pleasant -- not a bad feeling did I experience
Yet all this is gone, never to return.
A day of days never to enter my heart again.
My laughter is just yesterday's laugh
My thoughts yesterday's
Yet I am hoping that yesterday's day will be today's forever.

341

Manhattan Transfer/Edit

July 21, 1988

Things I believe about Bert:

He has strong beliefs about life and people.

As a friend he puts your needs and problems above his own.

His writing comes from deep within his very soul and represents his inner most feelings.

He can be counted upon in any situation as so few people can these days.

His commitment to life is strong and complete, as is so often the case when one has a "close call" with death.

Manhattan Transfer/Edit

Page 2.

I believe he realizes that life is more than mere work and existance. It is loyalty to family, friends, and self. It is leading others by example, not by shallow rhetoric.

Finally, I think Bert understands the meaning of love of his fellow beings. Even though we're all equal on this planet, he can, with his words, enlighten, inspire and guide some of us to a more enjoyable way of life.

Thanks Bert.

Howie Burch

WHAT I HEARD

I heard a sound
A slight thrill
A warm tingle
My throat was tight
No talk could prevail
Want for tears
Joy!
Happiness!
of knowing
What I heard.

Its string section
was the tin honk
the low bottom
Of its strings was bottomless
Music was created
Strings of gold.

The roar
The noise
Its sound
not coarse or harsh
Yet commanding
Conquering
Demanding to be heard
All listened, as each ear perked up
Delivery of their sound.

The music man
Like a cat on a hot tin roof
Ever entertaining
Ever capturing
Oh so "Bloody Good"
His voice shrill and sweet
His arms and legs marching with each chord
His "little face" a touch of genius
upon that platform in the sky.

The bank of music
Did create
Did mold
Three little black coffees
Their sound delightful and refreshing
Creation, a dream
All will acclaim this, as the band of rock.

What I hear
Will not dissipate
Or vanish in the space of time
All will gather
All will listen
To the marching of our peoples
With their cry "Hey Doctor"
A sound of world renown, all will acclaim.

THE WORST HAS PASSED

When the summer passes and the leaves fall to the ground,
The luster of green finds itself with a dull beauty.
To some this is their beauty,
While others find theirs has past.
This is just the way of life
Each day that goes by,
The worst has past,
And only a brighter future can there be.
These past few lines are just a few aspects of life,
You have seem many
Some you have touched, been a part of,
Battled and conquered many,
Yet the greatest one of your life is coming before you.
Weak you are not,
Strong -- like you bore four gifted children
Strong -- to find a man like your husband,
In all, strength because of yourself.
All must die with time
As one dies, they forever live on,
In our hearts, mind and children,
They can never die.
You are like a sturdy tree in the wind
swaying with each gust,
unknowing, but confident to endure this great ordeal.
You have shown what strength really is.

LEARN LOVE FROM DEATH

Suddenly it happened
Without warning
No notice.
Or reason why
But it did -
Her death

I still call her number,
Not realizing
She is no longer
She is, no - oh no,
It has troubled me
She is distant
Not even a speck - gone

I never knew
How much
It was
Until it was gone

Oh such a fool am I
I did love and never knew.

Her daring, captivating self
Will be a seed with me forever.
This little seed has grown and bloomed.
The ways of her shall become mine
And I will always guard them
For myself.

I have learned through her death
What love is
I pray, if this feeling
Should come forth again,
I must smother it during life
not death
And reap all its harvest.
I will give of myself,
Ever hoping I will not learn
of love from death.

DEATH ITSELF

The springs of summer are coming out of their nests,
For all flowers of beauty are taking a glance at summer.
While the trees prime for the capture of man
Voices of the brook sing loudly.
The mirror picture of life is here
But my friend can not see the summer of summer anymore
The bird's song is no longer heard to him
My friend has died. My friend so young.
Peace has come to him.
The living mourn, as their suffering lingers on
The world of being and pureness, is for the dead to see
I pray your memory will be everlasting in myself
Losing you is death itself.

AFFAIR OF LIFE

How does one such as I
feel
desire
want
an affair of my life?

How did it happen?
What created it?
Why,
For such an astute person
    as I?
To have this affair of my life
My desires are the same
Yet, there is a different feeling,
a wanting
of warmth
of talk
of need
Besides all that, I have
    riches of man.

My family
My love
My work
each is king of kings
Yet this affair of life
    is a sure desire.
But, what if...
No, but it could be
One sided
Without any feeling or desire
    on her part,
Just mine.

Yet, this affair of mine
may be only in my mind
never, to escape
the real desire
or explosion.

Yet, my thoughts are of
    gentler wants, of
caressing thoughts,
of love
This affair of life.

Oh, I've found it
This Eve, is she
She has touched my heart
Within my desires is that
  of Bobby
My life
My whole existence of being
for she is my love and the
    one affair of my life.

TO HAVE LOVED, THEN NOT AT ALL

Like the sip of rare wine
With its temperature just cooling,
Its taste, so ever wanting its flavor,
So is your love to me.
Love is not a word,
It is a feeling
of wanting
desiring
needing
one, so everlasting.

If this love should touch my eyes,
My soul
If, even for a moment, it would turn
into a decade.
Never, letting it escape my thoughts
and needs,
My appetite would be forever
bottomless,
Ever hungry for your love in return.
To this, I have loved,
If only for a picture dream,
Then to have never loved at all.

THE DEFEATED

We each try to reach the sun
But its rays graze our eyes
Always wanting to shade ourselves

We struggle through our life
Stop at each sign
Ever hoping, the want to win
to be first
No one cares for a loser
They only remember the Number One.

The work one performs
The deceiful attacks
The benefits of failings
All seem
Conquering you
But you move
On forward to
The hope of win

Each one deserves
In his Life
The Dream
To taste defeat

But to conquer
Sureness
Many reach the play of second
Few reach the continued taste of
being a winner.

With each winner
There is a loser.
Yet what of that person?
Is he not human?
Does he cry, or is he too
wise and old to do so?
Yet the rainfall of tears
clears the heart
And captures life anew
Ever knowing that "The
Defeated"
Shall be the one to rise again
only to
Taste the ever sweet feeling
Of being number one, the Winner.

ALL THE SAME

All of us look and hear
    the same.
We see loveliness of warmth
The ugliness of sorrow
    yet!
Your face is different, not
the same as any,
Not one exactly the same.
We gain together -- only to know
We are the same

Your voice I understand
I recognize
    yet!
Not two the same.

The whisper of the wind
The slam of a door
The talk of a child
The soul of desire, was one the same
A voice never equal to another's true
feelings, we are the same.

Does one not wonder
Each of us
    together
Different in looks and sound
Yet the same
    in feelings
    desires?
One must know

That God made us from one seed
Scattered over a vast plain
Some cold some hot
Yet the final place for all is the
    same.

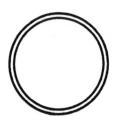

HER KISS

Her lips so soft and sweet
The caress of mine to hers
A chance for love to bloom with each embrace
Only her kiss to make love everlasting.

THE AIR OF DEFEAT

The swiftness of the wind
The quietness of death
Spread this air of defeat.

Was this the end?
Or the start
  of a beginning?

Many look
Stop!!
And relinquish
But yours is just a beginning.

There is no ominous touch about you
No dejection
For a loss to turn into victory.
Like a bird song -- its sweetness your
  rhapsody.
We look --
Past
Present
And to the future.
The road is seen
As if under a rainbow
The colors gleaming -- touching you --
In the air of defeat is the smell of
  success.

A TRAGEDY OF LIFE

This day is a little stranger than most days
The sun is shining like many a day, but for
  one there is no sunshine
Her laughter has turned to tears
A brilliant smile she once had; now shadowed
  by shame and sorrow
In the midst of darkness a shadow did appear,
Without a thought or warning
Your mind did dwell with fear
A sudden grasp for help; a gun; a blast; a
  killing
You look at the person with a frightful stare
Your love, your husband, is dead
Oh such an astute woman you once were,
But with this unforseen tragedy, you life
  has changed
The many inveigled attacks of strangers you
  did sustain
Your friends gather at your side; slowly in
  your need
The darkness of your thoughts has conquered many
As time moves on, may the enhancement of life
  touch you once more.

TO REMEMBER

Each day time goes by,
I try to remember
to be thankful for
the seeing of the trees
the smell of the air
the touching of a woman's love
the hearing of the birds
the warming of my heart
for all to hear
Thank You.

The opportunity is given me
the struggle
the sadness
the joy
the love
I shall remember,
I shall gather these memories
Cherish them
til death.

TO LEAVE A HOUSE OF LOVE

My home is my captivating desire of contentment.
To me, a den of warmth and cheer,
A place where love overflows in my heart,
Within its door, happiness and despair are not strangers.
My home is so pleasing to my every whim,
A place where dignity and repect are always seen.
A smile never given in a precarious way.
The thoughts of love, I always remember.

My home where each room is a heartfelt rhapsody
Each color picturesque, like the heaven above.
The floor soft and warm under my tired feet,
All this is my kingdom of happiness.

My home, If I were to leave,
A word could not be spoken for my grief,
The tears would not come to my eyes;
As all would be gone, in this life of mine.

FAREWELL MY FRIEND

Farewell my friend. As we drift apart,
Distant lands will separate our friendship;
Miles are our only enemy.
My friend I will remember you.
The fair times we had I cherish,
The bad times are not worthwhile memories.
Some say, "Friendship is gold",
You, my friend, make me feel richest of all.
May the carefree wonders of life come before you,
May the mirror picture of health be yours,
May jealous schemes leave your heart,
For what I possess, we both shall share.
The time has come to say goodbye,
A bottom-less feeling conquers my thoughts,
Knowing that our meeting will never be.
All I can say is goodbye.

YEARS TOGETHER

Enough time has passed in each one's life
To see what has happened:
Trying to forget, or
Remembering from morn till dusk
The bad with the good
The laughter with the sad
Good times with despair
Only to achieve one goal.
The years together move on for many
Yet, for us
Create life.

Remembering the tears through one
window pane
Comfort through our beloved
Distance revives our thoughts.
Without you, springs of summer cease
Treat of cotton candy has no flavor
The taste of wine turns to water.
Through strain and stress
Foreclosures on one's life
Your relief to me
Is the sweetest medication of life.
And now the pages in the book
Can be worn and torn
Dirty and ugly
But life with you, like all the years,
Grows fresh and true.

Each one that passes
A new happening occurs
Life for itself
Its true meaning
Of love and spirit
Of love of heart

This picture brown, that glows on me
Each hour of the day
Each day of my life
Through the years that bring
　My Dearest Little One.

NEVER THEIR OWN MEN

All of us struggle for survival in life.
Some are fortunate
to achieve
A pinnacle of glamor
or success of one kind
or another
Yet, most - -
I wonder!

I never question
That the sun will appear
or the sky is blue white
or the mountains are hard
and cold.
Yet, I wonder at these people.

Are they men
Or are they - "Never their Own"
Oh such words, said
With strong feelings
Yet true to the core.

Never could they achieve
Without others
Never could they do.
Without others
And never are they
Their own men.

Such a sorry task But that is life
From first day till tomorrow
Never to change.
Power, money survive all
And, men like these never to be
    "Their Own Men"

A MAN I MET

Yesterday, and tomorrow's yesterdays,
I met many men and women
With faces that are blank
But for a casual hello
Or a quick goodbye.

This given choice was mine
Large crowds and waves
    of people always there,
Never noticing anyone specific.

Today, yes, today
was the day of days
I met this man
who appears to be granite
Outside as well as inside
    his body.

Yet, as I see through his eys,
He is gentle
soft and caressing to his loves.
He fears none.
He sleeps without fear
    and loves without regret.

In this world of ours- with faults
    and hate
This man comes to light.
We learn from his thoughts.
We learn with respect through his ideas
He is man among men,
One who can never cast the first
    stone.

For he knows his shortcomings
and knows the reflections of life
But always
he will be his own,
This man I first met.

YOUR NEW LIFE

Years have passed
Through your life
Never having any meaning
Never noticed
The want of life taken for granted
Yet, your new life is seen.

Soon your task will encompass
Many struggles
Many happy moments
And just one love.
The two of you are ready to set up camp
Your new life is seen.

The camp of life together
Doing and wanting
Together
Each minute shall be a
distance
Each hour a week
Each thought a story
Doing and being two,
 yet
Conquering as one
Your new life is seen.

As this life appears,
Grab it, caress it,
Cherish it
For it is yours to have and hold.
It can disappear just as
It came.
Please know when you have gold
This gold is you two.
Your love
Your wanting
Your despair
Your health
Your needs
Alone, only your
Feelings for each other
These can be taken
Away only by yourselves
Never hesitate.

This is
Your new life.
Guard it and love it
It loves you both.

OUR FEELING

As the springs of life appear,
the reflections tell me
it is mine and mine only
this vicarious experience.
A feeling to me only,
Happy for such a
    delight of life.
If only for that my
    mind is free,
never to feel any
    response from anyone.

It happened suddenly
without warning.
A feeling of wanting and needing
Yet, why?
My eyes touched her,
My heart captured her
through my thoughts.
From this
I feel brand new,
    thanks to her.

363

A PASSING YEAR

Each year that passes one learns what life is.
To some the years pass quickly,
To others slowly and motionless.
With each year one must look for a better year to come,
And hope that the one past was not just a year in print,
But one of life full of its careless wonders,
Its tears filled with contentment after the storm.
The feeling of belonging -- wanting to give love and
    ever hoping for its return.
A notice of nature's rhapsody of life.
Its still beauty ever present before one's eyes.
Wanting to touch the knowledge of the world.
Yet never once afraid if ignorance should exist for a moment.
All this is present in life.
Every minute, hour, and day that passes.
A wanting to be with it; the hope it will be no stranger.
Yet the greatest look to the year that past,
Is your family.
The love they have given you, with responding efforts on
    your part.
To know and ever be dubious of their love,
Understanding, wisdom, care and devotion they have brought.
A smile and yet at times a frown they did entertain on
    your behalf.
All this has and will never pass.
And when you shall find your love.
He shall be within your heart,
And part of everything you do.
Then as the years shall drift
A tear, not of sorrow, but of thanks,
To know only wonderful years are to come.

MUST IT BE

Everything in the world
Is based on impression
Never mind how superb it may be
But what, how and why
Each impression is
Must it be this way?

When a man is down
Not in money
But in a state of mind
His loved ones
Are afraid of what others might say,
Do or feel
Must it be this way?

His love for them is true
He needs their love even more
When his mind captures all
His every thought - even when talking.
laughing with others
Never stopping
But only a fine thought
A touch
A caress
A sight of light for love
For his hope
Of a systematic ear
Usually secondary
Because his loved ones only
Want his strength
Never his despair or weakness
Why must it be this way?

He is a being
He cries
He laughs
He loves
Times he needs
More than ever - Her
Yet sharp tones given to somebody
Twice that of a knife
If only small pellets
Of that of a snow flake
Upon one's cheek

Its wetness soft
Light with warmth
To a gentle person
This must be to him

He needs the love
The affection
The wanting
Yet what must he do
The coldness is there
Still
As a twig in the forest.
Oh! for only
The small affection
It must be for him

His mind is puzzled
Not knowing what to do
Yet the denial
Only
For her love
Her understanding
And patience - - -
Must be for him.

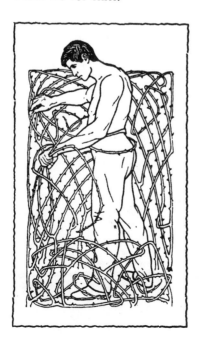

HOW DO I TELL YOU?

How does one such as I
tell you?
Tell you that when we first met
my life changed,
only you know that we can never be together
Never talk
Never love
Yet always in my thoughts
My ache for you is seen,
always wanting to capture your love
But how does one such as I
    tell you how I feel?

If I could talk,
my thoughts and desires are of you.
Your lovely wave to say "Hi"
Your funny, silly laugh,
Your Beauty Mark touch on your lip
The movement of your quiet but
    sure body.
Only wanting to caress it
Cherish and desire yours with mine.
Oh, if I could tell you.

My voice is silent.
My thoughts live
For the day that I could say
    I love you and want you.

HOW DO I LOVE THEE!

How do I love thee
That my thoughts are only of thee
When the sun rises from its sleepy nest
and peeks through
To arrest all with its warmth
My day begins
With the first morsel of air
to my body
My thoughts of my life with you
Fruitful
Daring
Loving
Enticing
Yet, how do I love thee?

A tree with its head to bloom
Into a lusty fruit
Making nature's dream come true
Its lust for life, captures all
Waiting for the rape of man
To show what it has
And what it is capable of.
This you have brought me
A companionship second to none
Except to God
Our years together have been real
Smooth and soft
At times, hard and coarse
Only caressing
to one another.
Your love I can not share
It only can be for me
Felt only with the heart
The cold has made it bearable
The warmth has made it life
Without the love
There is no song
No tomorrow
And never a today
With your love
There will always be a future
And a beyond
How do I love thee?
Is my life itself.

TO LOVE

To love you
is to want you

To have you
is to love you

Oh, love is you

If death shall come
before the twilight of life
I will have lived
for I have loved thee during life
And death shall be a joining
For my love shall prevail after death.

EXPOSED TO YOU

Your thoughts are so different from mine
But your kindness
Touches my heart
Creates a tingle
Like life's exposure to me
Knowing
Having someone such as you,
Life's true pleasure,
you.

WITH YOU

With you, no task can I not endure
No shore can I not conquer
No feeling can I not assume
No chance can I not accept.
With you, all life will not seem strange
No task too little
No fear so dark
Each light of life
A hope
A challenge
Not only for despair
but hope
of being
With you, for today,
tomorrow
And year after year,
Enduring, creating
Conquering
Each year
Each span
As life moves on
With you and I
As one.
Forever, till
Tomorrow's tomorrow
Disappears
forever.

I LOVE THEE

Seeing my love once more is a dream come true,
For beauty and love unfolds from the heart;
Her voice is sweet as that of the golden harp.
As myself, a slave to her only.
My love, My love, I do love thee.
When you cry my heart yearns to comfort you,
Your smile of happiness, is happiness to me.
I would love thee till almighty God permits -
And then in immortality.
To hear your voice, is love within my heart.
I love thee, as the earth loves her children.
To hear her say, "I love thee," has made my dream a
    reality.

THE SEA OF GRASS

As I sit down to rest, my eyes perceive
A large field of tall grass.
Its pale color catches the air
As the wind blows to the east and west.
Fields of tall grass sway with each gust
The waves of grass reach the shore.
My sea of grass touches me.

LOVE ME JUST A LITTLE

As the morning sun enters my room
Its warmness captures my sleep
Awakening to this world of happiness of tears
New days are to enter my life since I've met my love.
In my dreams you have always been distant but there.
At times one could hear me shout "I Love You"
Yet can one such as I love
By this I mean, afraid -- what it might be
Tis true when we first met all went.
My thoughts of all wordly beliefs dissolved
You were my life.
I would succeed from that moment on
No task could not be mastered.
All were easy to conquer
The will was here
The stage was set and only the asking,
    "To love me just a little."

GOODBYE FOR NOW

Our friendship has been short, but pleasing.
Your dramatic ideas I wish to capture
The sincere dry manner of your talk.
Feeling of belonging, I do have with you,
This atmosphere one cannot forget.

You travel over a deep dark ocean,
The land you seek different from mine
Their ways of life symbolic to you and me
But one can be sure that their ways of companionship
   are the same,

My friend, I will miss you.
My Goodbye for now
Will be my Hello for tomorrow.

374

TO LOSE ONES LOVE

Each year that passes I do yearn for your love.
The whisper of your name,
Your gentle hand through my hair
A reality comes forth; your earthly love is gone.

Time is to be the healer of all,
Time can never end love.
An emptiness of heart I do feel
For one has taken my love, never to be replaced by another.

A WORD

Your place in the world is seen
Fame and wealth await your touching.
I fear you think this unreal.
Learn the world is coarse; yet fear not
    the ominous touch of it.
For each of us walks in our own footsteps.
At times we feel alone and wanting.
For the word of life is new to you.

Letter from Cyndi Lauper

I've read ~~many~~ a few books in my time, and this is one of them.

♡

Cyndi Lauper

Madonna- Her show in Wembly, England

HANDS TO HEAVEN

The ground was moving
The stars sparkled
It was not an earthquake,
nor a storm
The waves of hands to heaven

They felt free as the air
Smooth as a baby's rear cheek
The aroma as fresh cut grass
Desireable as a woman's need
This, the hands of heaven.

I shall never forget the feeling
  for love and desire
This bestowed upon me
She captured one's heart
One's soul
The need to be part of the crowd
Stronger were the claps
Each clap an inspiration.

Moving on
Louder
Stronger
Yet, not harsh
As the softness of love.

In rhyme and rhythm
The hands of heaven
Were like an act of God
Bestowed upon her
For a vision and sign.

Thank you! For being "Madonna"

Letter from Freddie Gershon

May 31, 1988

Bert Padell
1775 Broadway
7th Floor
New York, N.Y. 10019

THE OFFICE

Dear Bert,

I'm walking down 57th street smiling, a bounce in my step, Tony Manero in the opening sequence of SATURDAY NIGHT FEVER. People look dour and incredulous at the silly grin fixed on my face.

I just left your office. How terrific I felt -- How good. You were my Proustian catalyst, a rememberance of things past, when the candy store was the magic kingdom and I was a kid over-whelmed by how much there was to look at, touch and ask for. Your office is an island of whimsy & fun in a business ocean of greed and avarice.

You've created a fantasmogoric hodge podge of wonderfulness with silly goodies and treasures combined in different styles, modes, periods and tastes to envelop the visitor in a sanctuary from the real world.

So, there you are Bert, wallowing in your eclectic array of "tschakas", telling the story behind each, with warm and loving descriptions of the friends and clients behind each story. You care about them. You ooze compassion. You become excited and animated gesticulating in genuine delight with your wonders and your memorabilia.

I find yourenthusiasm infectious, my blood surges, my adrenalin's going--. I'm out of your office, I'm on the street, but your magic stays with me as I bounce back into the real world, protected for a while by the recollection of our visit.

An office so refreshingly spontaneous and honest and unique... just like you.

What an office!

What a guy!

Your pal,

Freddie Gershon

Letter from David Frank

Dear Burt;

Thanks for everything your've done for us. There is no one that
compares to you. You are accountant, mamager, advisor, uncle, father,
brother, but most of all you are a caring, understanding friend.

Thanks again ~~Best~~

Sincerely

David Frank

OUR LADY

How strong she stands in the wind
Each gust blowing, but not a hair
    out of line
Her stern but adorable look
opening her eyes to us
Pouring her heart, daring us to come
A chance worth while

She says
Never a frown or a despairing look
Our Lady in the Wind.

The symbol of hope
Charity and love
Her welcome lamp yearning for all to see
Never a challenge
Only beacon shining in perpetuity
This our Lady in the wind.

Never disparaging
Never disappearing
Never a frown
Never a no
Always arms welcome
This is our Lady.

TO SAY GOODBYE

My dear ones, It is hard at this time
to bid farewell
I have loved you all, for all my life
From the first sight, happiness did appear
Love did enter my mind and heart
And now strange thoughts and deeds
did conquer me.
Please forgive me I did not want this
Or ever in my wildest dreams did I think it
would happen to me
Fair it is not, just it is not!
Love is the only thing keeping me going
Yet, Goodbye.

WHO IS ALEX?

Who is he?
He is love
He is your dream
He is your wanting
Your desire
Your need
Your spring
The music of life
The brook of cool running water
Searching to touch us all
This be Alex
Wherever he might be
His tones
His sounds of the music
Touch your heart
   and ear
For this be Alex
A man of love and care
We love you
God, oh God
Be with you forever.

CHALLENGE OF OUR LIFE

Tragedy did occur
It was sudden, sadly seen
Yet they, those who lost
Were not lost
Remembered by us all
Our challenge of our life
They shall more to come
It shall be done
For us all
This challenge of our life
We shall search
The sights of God
The challenge shall disappear
The reality of their loss
Shall be our gain,
Thanks to them
The Challenger VII

NOTTVRNO

385

TRUE INNOCENCE

My eyes look into space
And time
And wonder
What have I done
And why?

Do I deserve what I have;
Am I what I think I am?
I do believe sincerely
All of us are one.
No evil
Loyalty for all.
I deal with true love from within
Appearances are one thing
But what matters
Is the inside of the person.
Does he have
The true innocence?

SAVE YOUR FRIENDSHIP

Friendship, is a needing
A wanting
A giving
Of one to another
To remember when one needs
Or wants.

A memory of a place for love
To have you part of it
All this one must caress
Care and cherish
Save your friendship
Don't spread it to many
Or share it- because it is your
Friendship.

ALONE

The smoke was thick
The air didn't move
Still
Noisy
You were there
The crowd
Yet, you were alone!

TALKING WORDS

We hear
request
desire and
most of all, want
the right words -
The sounding of them
to be pure and real
Talking words -

I want truth
no compromise
no deceptions
but, the words
So I can know
and realize
you are just not
Talking words -

No falsehoods
that your word is
smooth and pure
There is only one thing
we all have,
Nobody can take it away from us
Our word -
Words of love
peace and security
from me to you.

GROWING OLD

The year's transcend
into decades
Yet I feel sincere
to myself- my body and soul.
My mind is clean and clear
The year's disappeared in a mist.

Is it a sense of mind?
Or feeling!
Yet, I want the years to grow
Gracefully
To be wanted and needed
I am growing old.
Still remembering the good times
Going forward to the future
Forgetting the bad,
Remember my youth
And looking forward to growing old,
Which is oh, so good.
I will remember my past thoughts
As I will all of yesterday's dreams
Today and tomorrow I will look
Forward to
Growing old

I WANT TO BELIEVE

Through life we reach high
for the greater treasures.
To some, money is the power
To some, love and dearest
is the strength of life.
Yet, I look to see and feel
You a friend that is to be desired.
And I want to believe.
Can it be so?

THE END AND THE BEGINNING

Something ends
when
Something begins!
Why?
Is this the role of life
Did God make this happen?
Did man make this occur
Or is this life
The toll we all have to bear
Or is it a toll?
Because, this is life
The chance for all of us
to begin and start
While others rest
And begin again
The start and end of life!

I THOUGHT IT WAS YESTERDAY

The days transcend into life
Not knowing, why? Or what?
I am in a dilemma
Ever wondering
Desiring
What
Where
Oh!!
I thought it was yesterday.

June 21, 1988

Bert,

To the man who got me started
thank you for helping me
live the dream. I'm having
the time of my life.

Health, Happiness & Prosperity
Your friend,

Franke Previte
and
Oscar.

L. PETER PARCHER

500 FIFTH AVENUE

NEW YORK, NEW YORK 10110

BERT PADELL

Bert Padell is a swell guy - swell is a word that was
in vogue in the 40's and hasn't been heard much of
since, but that's the way Bert is -- he's like a
1940's New York guy: straight ahead, sincere, tough but
kind, no frills, hard working, uncommonly loyal, a
family guy, the kind of fellah that once he is your
friend he is your friend for life, the kind of guy
whose word is his bond and whose handshake you take to
the bank. I'm glad he's my pal but I wish he wrote
poetry better.

L. Peter Parcher

June 27, 1988

SENSE OF EXCELLENCE

We try to achieve
Try to do
What all of us, look to
A place
A time
In the sun
To be the best
The winner
The achiever
Number One
In all respects
This is a sense of excellence
Yet, then again, what is excellence

XMAS, IS A FRAME OF MIND?

Yet, the snow has yet to touch my face
And the reindeer are ready for
the big start
Is that day coming?
No -
Because it is not just a smile
a happy saying
a present
a frame of mind
This shall conquer us for all year round
To love thy neighbor
To love thy wife
To adore thine child
To respect thy enemy
To love thy God
but, best of all to have feelings that the
Xmas spirit is all year within thy mind
and soul of us all

I have a dream for all to feel
free from thought and love and best of all
to feel free from within, that this feeling
is Xmas all year round!

HOMEBOY

I am what I am
Yet, I will never forget my roots
of my space, my neighborhood
The place some shun or look away from
It is where I was born
lived
and learned
Where we bloomed without compromise
Without despair
Without the dollar
My place
My need
I am this Homeboy.

MAN'S BEST FRIEND IS MAN

He is called Man's best friend
He is always there in time of need
There in time of despair
There for cheer
There for love
There for you
Yet best of all, he is Man's best friend
That is Man!!

TO BE REAL

To be what God asked you to be
To be Real,
To yourself
To your mind
Your body, your being
Never afraid of a shadow
Shadows don't exist
Foul weather never seen.
Real is what we all try to achieve
Some never make it
While few succeed
They are the few
and beautiful
Real to them
Real inside
And, Real to life.

LITTLE IS ENOUGH

To have you for a day
is better than not at all
Yet, to touch your cheek
See your smile
Hear your voice
Smell your scent
Love you- only love you
Even if just a little
Is better to have loved thee a little,
Only to have loved.

Letter from Michael Murphy of the group– The System

His Pen.

His Pen, an instrument
he uses it, he thinks.
It never went to college and yet its filled with knowledge
His Pen, an instrument
his signature is bent n.
He's on the phone again, tryin to educate with
common sense
His pen, an instrument
he holds with confidence like Hendryx played guitar
    and Hiefetz the violin
His pen, an instrument he talks to it i bet
when searching for the answer to questions raised
across his desk
His pen an instrument it came down from the heavens
I know he's always had one since the day he was (11)
eleven.
His pen an instrument his desk his loyal steed
He races off to battle to fight for you and me.!!

Letter from Kurtis Blow

Bert
    I want to thank you for sticking by me through the Hard times. You were one of the only people who believed that I never lost it. People like you are so hard to come by and I wish there were. thanks again for all of the Support and I will never forget what you've done for me.

          Sincerely yours

            Kurt Blow

WEARING A MASK

Is it a comedy?
or is it tragedy?
The wearing of the masks
have come about thru years of time
Yet has the opportunity for all
been bestowed upon us all
Or are we wearing masks to choose.

To choose from all walks of life
Whatever one might want
never to be blinded
from what is out there
Then again we all choose right and wrong!

Then tear off the mask
when playing a game
Because life is not one.
The chance
The opportunity
The beginning
The start
Must be available to us all

Masks are for games
Not for real, true people
of substance.
The only thing we have in life
Is the opportunity to choose
based upon the true feeling
and ability of the person
Not of one, what does the name sound like
Or is his skin, what color?
Or his beliefs, what!!
But of him we must choose, and what he
can do and accomplish
for it is the face of the person
for the person and by the person
we should choose
that is what God intended, and did
so the wearing of the masks are in the dust
and only such a game for make believe.

SHOULD HAVE

The place where I live
The time of each day
Wanders away
Wondering
Hoping
Dreaming
Shall I have dared
or
Shouldn't I have
Is one puzzlement.
Is one question
To question life itself
or its meaning
Should I have done
or shouldn't!

BE FRIENDS

They told me
You will like him

We met
Time passed
I do love him.

But now
They are both part of me
Do you think they can be friends?

I love them both
My father and you
My dear new husband.

ME

It is not what I achieve
It is what I have been forced to accept
God, Why?
Me!!!
Then again
Why not me?

A DINNER WITH FRIENDS

The place was dazzling
The atmosphere beyond a dream
Being with the best of my life
Five dear friends
To welcome in another year of age
With you my friend and lover wife
Two lovely dear couples
To make my life worth living
And waiting for
Another year
A dinner with friends.

STONE FACES

The sun shone
down on us.
We did not squint
or hide from the
rays.
You will know that
some day we
would be
Stone Faces.
Did we only have
To look forward
to this?
Or was there more!
A hereafter?
It was so
that tomorrow would
be a beginning-
And the stone Faces
would just
be memories not to be
forgotten.

Letter from Henry Frommer

CHARTER FINANCIAL, INC.
Merchant Bankers

HENRY FROMMER
President

September 15, 1988

Mr. Bert Padell
Padell, Nadell, Fine, Weinberger & Co.
1775 Broadway
New York, NY 10019

Dear Bert:

I am delighted to tell you that Alan Fischer and our colleagues will be taking a table at the November 4th dinner honoring you for your humanitarian work in the field of diabetes. Unfortunately, because of a prior conflict with another charitable institution, I will not be able to attend. I therefore wanted to offer you my sincere congratulations. No one who has worked with you as I have all these years can doubt the appropriateness of this honor that is being bestowed upon you. Your standards of ethics and humanity have always been maintained at the highest level even in a world where daily activities make it so easy to cast these standards aside. It is good that you are being honored, but the real honor must be reserved for those who have had the privilege of knowing you and working with you. I count myself among these fortunate ones. On behalf of my wife and myself may I again offer you sincere congratulations.

Yours truly,

HF:mr

12:53

REPUBLIC NATIONAL BANK OF NEW YORK

1180 AVENUE OF THE AMERICAS · NEW YORK, N.Y. 10036　(212) 840-1088
TELEX 234967　　　　　　　　　　　　　　　　CABLES: BLICBANK NEW YORK

JAMES H. BUCK, JR.
VICE PRESIDENT

August 15, 1988

Mr. Bert Padell
Padell, Nadell, Fine & Weinberger
1775 Broadway
New York, New York 10019

Dear Bert,

The poem describing our dinner brings me great joy since I consider
you a friend in the true sense of the word.　In fact, I consider you
like family and I hope and pray we are healthy enough in the future
to continue our friendship together.

Very truly yours,

James H. Buck, Jr.
First Vice President

Dedicated to the American Diabetes Association

THE DISEASE, THAT IS SILENT!

Its affects touch many -- caress no one.
Needs no start up time.
It is quiet, unpretentious
It walks with kings and peasants
Neither crying or laughing
mean much to it.
Suffering, through time
despair occurs.
Strength and positive beliefs are
the only salvation.
Spears of courage
Handsome smiles overturn bad dreams
and thoughts.
This silent intruder prevails.
Ever sweeping and enduring
into areas "not wanted".
This silent disease.
We shall overcome!
We shall conquer!
We shall be forceful!
This silence shall be dead forever.
Forever.

TEARS IN THE RAIN

It falls upon with light drops
Its morsels deck our faces
It brings on sadness and grief at times
It also brings life and happiness
It has joy and candy treat.
It is a puzzlement!!
For this to bring two different feelings,
My touch of rain in tears.

RIGHT DOESN'T ALWAYS WIN

I think
knowing
I am right
Yet, I wonder
Does right always win?

1988 HUMANITARIAN AWARD DINNER

HONORING

BERT PADELL

NOVEMBER 4, 1988 • THE PIERRE HOTEL

AMERICAN DIABETES ASSOCIATION
NEW YORK DOWNSTATE AFFILIATE, INC.

To Bob DeNiro

I FOUND YOU

Through life we experience
roads of light and despair
Yet my light has come through
you. I've found
Or have we found each other!

Like a streak in the night
that follows the storm
As quiet as it appeared
when the calm has set in
the reflection of my friendship
Is indispensable
Even dearing
By far in lasting perpetuity

To have one for each other
Is a God's gift
A friendship to endure us
till death and beyond.

BAD DREAMS

I moved back and forth
side to side
Only to wonder
Why?
Do I think and feel this way
I will try and ever hope
that the sea of uneasiness disappear
So that all my bad dreams are no longer

Why do they come?
Why do they enter my mind
Despair- unhapiness is the only answer
Yet I will ruffle all the dreams of badness
To make calm seas
Tropical rivers
Lovely smelling gardens
for my dreams for the future
will only have aroma's of the rose
kept new and tall
For good dreams shall only prevail.

THANKFUL FOR WHAT WE HAVE

When you sleep
without pain
We all take this "as is"

Yet I don't have it
Am I different
Or is it unfair?

The pain only stops
with pills and liquid taken
Relief for a while
Sometimes
A day
hours
minutes or even a minute

When I was straight without pain
I took everything for granted
Never realizing what it
would be with the pain
If I get another chance
I look and hope that I will be thankful
for what I have
A life without pain.

413

LOVE

Is it you
Is it me

Entwined into one
Till God asks us to
    leave each other

To meet again,
    someday soon
And soon could be
    tomorrow or sometime

Love.

I MUST WRITE HIM A NOTE

I must write him a note
and tell him why
love and cherish all the times
gone by

I must write him a note
and tell him of all the good times
and bad ones too!!
Yet, I love thee for all
the times
I want him all the time
I must write him a note to
tell you this,
my darling love.